The
ASCETICAL LIFE

by

PASCAL P. PARENTE,

S.T.D., PH.D., J.C.B.

Associate Professor of Ascetical Theology
Catholic University of America

✝

B. HERDER BOOK CO.
15 & 17 SOUTH BROADWAY, ST. LOUIS 2, MO.
AND
33 QUEEN SQUARE, LONDON, W. C.
1947

INTRODUCTION

Ascetical and mystical writings form a large portion of Christian literature. In asceticism, as in so many other fields, the increased number of books on the subject has not always succeeded in advancing the spiritual science itself. However, the present century with its grim and ugly realities of wars and destruction is turning with a growing interest to the study of ascetical and mystical problems, bringing to it a system and methods often ignored in the past. Yet the very difference in method employed in these studies is responsible for the appearance of two principal schools in ascetical and mystical theology in our day: the descriptive and the speculative school.

The purpose of this book is to present in a concise and systematic treatise the fundamental principles of Christian asceticism, and also to bring a certain unity to this discipline by reconciling opposed opinions through opportune distinctions, whenever feasible. Special consideration is given to the teaching of the Fathers of the Church, whose testimony is often quoted at length.

The present volume treats of the ascetical life exclusively, not of the mystical life, which will require a second volume.

The need for a systematic course in ascetical theology was felt in the United States at the beginning of this century, and recommendation for its inclusion in the seminary curriculum was made as early as 1908 at Cincinnati

at the meeting of the Seminary Department of the Educational Association. Pope Pius X in his *Motu proprio* of
September 9, 1910,[1] reminded students for the priesthood
that one of the necessary sciences they should learn is
"the science of Christian piety and practice called ascetical theology." After the First World War, Pope Benedict
XV ordered that a chair of ascetical theology be established at the two principal theological schools in the city
of Rome. Finally Pius XI, in his encyclical *Deus scientiarum Dominus* (June 12, 1931), prescribed a course of
ascetical theology as a *disciplina auxiliaris* for all theological schools.

In the fall of 1938, ascetical and mystical theology were
introduced as a separate course in the School of Sacred
Theology at the Catholic University of America in Washington. When the author was called to lecture on the subject he realized that of the several textbooks available
none was quite adequate or concise enough. Encouraged
by the favorable reception of his Latin lectures on ascetical and mystical theology and often requested to make
them available to a wider circle, he decided to rewrite
them in English, adding many scriptural and patristic
texts and a general bibliography of ascetical and mystical
writers. The result is the present book, which is an introduction to the ascetical life and to the sources that offer
a wider and more comprehensive presentation of the subject. May it contribute to a deeper knowledge and to a
more fervent practice of the science of the saints.

PASCAL P. PARENTE
Catholic University of America

[1] A.A.S., II, 668.

CONTENTS

v

CONTENTS

CONTENTS   vii

CONTENTS

PART I

GENERAL ASCETICS

CHAPTER I

PRELIMINARY QUESTIONS

A. Meaning and History of the Word "Ascetic"

1. The word "ascetic" comes from the Greek verb *askein,* whence the nouns *askesis* and *asketes,* and the adjective *asketikos* were derived. During the Homeric period, the verb *askein* meant simply to fashion, to adorn, to work ingeniously. In the philosophic period that preceded Socrates, it meant to exercise, to practice, and it was applied to our spiritual faculties in the acquisition of virtue [1] and learning.[2] It also meant to practice an art or profession, to endeavor. It was during the Hellenic-Roman period that the absolute meaning of practicing and training prevailed, and the word *asketikos* was the equivalent of industrious, athletic. The Apostle St. Paul was the first to introduce this verb into Christian literature and give it a Christian "baptism" and meaning. The verb *askein* occurs in the Acts (24:16).Defending his innocence before Felix the governor, Paul said: "And herein do I endeavor (*asko*) to have always a conscience without offence towards God, and towards men." Here, for the first time, *askein* means a striving for Christian perfection, a perfection which is not merely exterior, like that of pagan philosophers in general, but first and above all an interior perfection and purity of conscience, a constant

---

1 Πλέονες ἐξ ἀσκήσιος ἀγαθοὶ γίγονται ἤ ἀπὸ φύσιος. Democr., *Frag.* 242.
2 Φύσεως καὶ ἀσκήσεως διδασκαλία δεῖτει. Protagoras, *Frag.* 3.

3

(always) endeavor and effort to keep that conscience
stainless before God and men. The athletic connotation
of the word was well known to St. Paul, who more than
once uses athletic concepts and words to convey ideas
of spiritual effort and practices (cf. I Cor. 9:24–27; Eph.
6:11–16; I Tim. 4:7 f.). His "endeavor," therefore, means
spiritual exercise, spiritual training. His words offer also
a beautiful definition of asceticism, which may be defined
as "the endeavor to have always a conscience without offence towards God and towards men."

2. Origen was one of the first ecclesiastical writers to
use the word "ascetic" to denote such Christians as observed perfect continence or virginity and devoted themselves to mortifications and austerities: "I shall relate what
is usually done by our ascetics." [3] In his *Contra Celsum*
(V, 49), he points out the difference between the Pythagoreans and the Christian ascetics: "See the difference of
motive for which the Pythagoreans and our ascetic abstain
from things that have life." The word *askesis* occurs frequently in the *Life of St. Anthony* written by St. Athanasius: "The more they [the devils] do such things to us,
the more fervently shall we devote ourselves to an ascetic
life" (chap. 30). Palladius in his *Historia Lausiaca* uses
the word *askesis* in describing the austere mode of life
of the various hermits and monks of Egypt whom he had
visited. He uses the term "ascetic" not only in the old
meaning of continence and virginity, but also in the sense
of austerities of every kind, the practice of virtues, prayer
itself. Speaking of Macarius, an Alexandrian priest, Palladius relates that "his asceticism consisted in imitating
whatever good work he heard performed by others; and

[3] Διαγράψω τι γινόμενον τοῖς ἀσκηταῖς (*Hom.* 20 *in Ier.*).

that another form of his asceticism was his striving to overcome sleep." [4] Of a certain monk named Paul, the same Palladius says that his work and asceticism consisted in praying continually.[5] It was at this time, during the fourth century of the Christian era, that the word "ascetics" began to denote the exercise of Christian perfection in general as a most certain way to eternal salvation. St. Basil says that the only purpose of the ascetical life is to take care of the salvation of our soul.[6] Consequently, at this early period, "asceticism" denoted the whole range of spiritual life, mystical contemplation and mystical phenomena not excluded, although a distinction seems to have been made between the ordinary ascetics, held to strict observance of religious rules, and the perfect ones, who needed no rule because they spent all their life in divine contemplation.[7]

3. In the second half of the seventh century, after the mystical works of Dionysius the Pseudo-Areopagite had become known and were accepted by Catholics, the term "mystical theology" began to replace "ascetics" in the designation of that same endeavor toward the attainment of Christian perfection. The word "ascetic" was not employed by Latin writers except sometimes as a transcription of the Greek. It was not used in the Middle Ages, and only in modern times was it adopted in Latin textbooks and in modern languages generally. In the seventeenth century, treatises on ascetical theology began to appear. But such works made no distinction between ascetical practices and mystical graces. So the *Theologia*

---

[4] *Hist. Lausiaca*, 18, 1, 3.
[5] *Ibid.*, 20, 1.
[6] *Sermones ascetici*, 2, 1.
[7] *Hist. Lausiaca*, 32, 7.

ascetica of P. Schorrer, S.J. (Rome, 1658), includes also the treatment of infused contemplation. A clear-cut distinction in the presentation of ascetical and mystical material was introduced in the eighteenth century. The work of G. B. Scaramelli, S.J.,[8] was found more practical and illuminating than any before. This new system of presenting the subject of spiritual science was the result of the writings of St. Theresa of Avila and St. John of the Cross on the one hand; and on the other hand the distrust with which mysticism was regarded for a while because of the condemned doctrines of Michael de Molinos (1627–96), Mme. Guyon (1648–1717), Father Francis LaCombe, Abbé Bertot, and others. We consider this new system a great contribution to the study of ascetical and mystical disciplines. Well understood, it opens the door to deeper and wider researches and to a genuine progress in the understanding of ascetical and mystical classics.

B. DEFINITION, SOURCES, DISTINCTIONS

4. In the preceding paragraphs we have noted the etymological definition of asceticism so far as it means a mode of life. The science which determines the nature of Christian perfection and the means of tending to it and attaining it is called ascetical theology. Ascetics, as a sacred science, may be defined as that part of sacred theology which, out of the sources of divine revelation and the infallible magisterium of the Church, derives the nature of Christian perfection and the various ways and means of tending to it and attaining it. Ascetical theology is a practical science; its purpose is to guide and direct the soul in the acquisition of Christian perfection, to make

---

[8] *Direttorio ascetico* and *Direttorio mistico.* Venice, 1754.

saints. Like every other part of sacred theology, it bases
its teaching first on the sources of divine revelation,
namely, Sacred Scripture, tradition, then on the Magisterium, that is, Church definitions and the common
teaching of the Fathers and the theologians. As a special
source for ascetical and mystical theology, we may add
the ascetical and mystical writings of saints and doctors
of the Church and the lives of the saints, as described in
the official process of their canonization. A firm adherence
to divine revelation and the common doctrine of the
Catholic Church is of primary importance because of
the many dangers of aberration in this field, as shown by
the numerous heresies and erroneous opinions that have
appeared in almost every century of the Christian era.

5. The purpose of almost every other course of theology is to impart a knowledge of revealed truth with
regard to faith and morals. When this knowledge blos-
soms into sanctity, we are in the field of ascetical and
mystical theology. This course is, therefore, a necessary
complement of dogmatic and moral theology. Since ascetical theology has a specific object of its own, which
may be called Christian perfection in theory and practice, it follows that this course is distinct from dogma,
moral, and all other subjects of theology. There is a perfect organic unity among all branches of theology. As
in a living body all the various functions are coordinated
and directed toward one supreme end, which is life itself, so in the body of sacred sciences the various subjects
are combined into a system with supernatural life for its
end, namely, God's life in us and our life in Him. Considering ascetical theology in relation to all other theological subjects, we must admit both unity with them all and

distinction from them, that is, organic unity and functional distinction. This is obvious in the case of dogma but less so in that of moral, for these reasons:

1) Moral theology, especially as expounded by St. Thomas in his *Summa theologica,* part 2, contains all the elements necessary for leading souls to Christian perfection.

2) Both moral and ascetics have a common object: human acts, precepts, counsels, theological and moral virtues.

3) Until recently, ascetical and mystical questions were contained in the ordinary course of moral theology.

Let us consider the second part first. It is true that, to a great extent, moral and ascetics have a common object, but it is only the material object that is common, not the formal object. The proper formal object of moral theology is the morality of human acts, the extent of the obligation of precepts and virtues; the formal object of ascetical theology is the perfection of the human acts, precepts, virtues, and counsels considered as means for the attainment of perfection. Sciences and habits are distinguished according to their formal objects, namely, that particular aspect in which the subject matter is viewed. Therefore a perfect distinction must be admitted between moral and ascetics.

Although moral theology, as expounded by St. Thomas in his *Summa,* contains the elements of perfection, it is not the province of moral theology to develop those elements, but of ascetics. Many of those elements are found also in dogmatic theology and originally in Scripture. Ascetical theology presupposes moral theology as well as Scripture and dogma. The fact that ascetics and mysticism were,

until recently, an appendix of the works in moral theology, is a circumstance to be regretted. It is well known
how little attention it received and how often it was completely omitted from the course. The *ratio studiorum* of
the Apostolic Constitution *Deus scientiarum Dominus* of
1931, places moral theology among the principal subjects
of a theological course, and ascetical theology among
auxiliary subjects. This fact should prove conclusively the
asserted distinction between moral theology and ascetics
not only for logical reasons but also for expediency of
method.

The distinction between pastoral theology and catechetics is evident from the formal object of these courses.
It is true that ascetics enters a little into both fields, but
this is because of the organic unity mentioned above,
and because of the fact that ascetics is almost like the
soul of the entire theological course, since every subject
should lead, directly or indirectly, to Christian perfection.

c. Methods

6. Ascetical-mystical theology is a practical science.
We have to deal with theological principles and with
ascetical facts and mystical phenomena. Two different
methods have been adopted through the centuries, the
speculative and the descriptive. The speculative, also
called deductive or doctrinal, consists in gathering into
a system the principles of spiritual life from the sources of
divine revelation and the teachings of theologians, and in
determining, by deduction, the nature of perfection, our
obligation of tending to it, and the various means to be
employed.

The descriptive method, called also experimental and

psychological, consists in observing and describing ascetical and mystical facts and phenomena in oneself or in others, in order to derive from them some general characteristics by which similar facts may be recognized and some clear and practical rules of conduct may be formulated.

7. Generally speaking, the speculative, or doctrinal, method was employed by the Fathers of the Church and the Scholastics; the descriptive or psychological method by the saints in relating and describing their own experiences. The early Fathers are satisfied with inculcating precepts, counsels, and rules of conduct, like the *Didache* (chapter 1, and part of chapter 3); St. Clement of Rome in his *Epistle to the Corinthians* (passim); Hermas in *The Shepherd* (one of the first attempts in combining the descriptive and the speculative method may be detected here); Clement of Alexandria in his *Paedagogus* (strictly doctrinal); St. Ambrose in his *De officiis ministrorum, De virginibus, De viduis;* St. Augustine particularly in his *Confessiones* and *Soliloquia* (a fusion of both methods, beautifully blended); Cassian in his *Collationes* (the descriptive method predominates, the doctrine being the fruit of the personal experience of hermits and monks). As a rule, when the Fathers base their teaching on their own experience, the mixed method is employed, otherwise the speculative method prevails. St. Thomas Aquinas, and after him the Scholastics generally, except St. Bonaventure, adopted the speculative method.

The great St. Theresa employed the descriptive or psychological method in all her ascetical and mystical writings. St. John of the Cross, as a great mystic and great theologian, employed the combined method; the same

must be said of St. Francis de Sales. The method followed
by Cardinal de Berulle and his school is speculative. Coming down to writers and authors of our own days, we have
the descriptive method beautifully represented in the
work *The Graces of Interior Prayer* by A. Poulain, S.J.
The speculative or deductive method is represented by
R. Garrigou-Lagrange, O.P., in his *Christian Perfection
and Contemplation*. It is true that the author recommends
the union of both methods (pages 21 ff.), but his whole
system is based on the scholastic speculative and deductive method. Father A. Tanquerey, S.S., in his *The Spiritual Life*, recommends and follows the combined method;
so does Father J. de Guibert, S.J., in his textbook, *Theologia spiritualis ascetica et mystica*.

Either method followed exclusively runs the danger of
becoming unscientific in the treatment of ascetical and
mystical theology. The speculative method, employed to
the exclusion of the descriptive or experimental, may run
the risk of drawing conclusions not supported by facts.
The descriptive, being concerned with facts and not with
theological principles, may end up in the realm of rational
psychology. Therefore a combined method must be followed. The facts and phenomena must be observed in
the light of theological principles, and these principles
must be studied and interpreted by taking into account
facts and phenomena.

D. IMPORTANCE OF ASCETICAL THEOLOGY

8. Some idea of the excellence, necessity, and importance of ascetical theology may be gained from what has
been said above in paragraphs 4 and 5, where we spoke
of the nature, the sources, and the place of ascetical

theology with respect to other theological disciplines. Its importance is also evident in the various names that have been attributed to it: the science of the saints because, first taught by the saints by word and example, it leads to sanctity; the art of perfection because it teaches in a practical way the highest and noblest of all perfections a man may wish for, the Christian perfection; the spiritual science, the queen of all sciences, which depends not only on the noblest in man but also on divine and supernatural factors for its results.

9. No man will ever become perfect in any art without being taught and shown how to work out the small details that spell beauty and perfection; without a guide and a teacher he will remain always a novice. Many faithful, among both the laity and the clergy, remain plain novices in spiritual life until they die, because they have never made a serious study of ascetical and mystical theology. This is to be condemned in a priest: by reason of his office, he is a spiritual teacher and guide. We shall not for a moment entertain the Platonic idea that man's moral worth is constituted largely by his knowledge, and that man attains perfection in proportion to his knowledge of the good. Much more than mere knowledge is required for Christian perfection, but knowledge is an indispensable requisite for its attainment.

10. St. Theresa of Avila speaks out of her own experience when she says: "Great damage was done to my soul by half-learned confessors; . . . but I was never deceived by one who was well informed." [9]

The study of ascetical and mystical theology is now obligatory for clerics. It is an introduction to the spiritual

[9] *Libro de la Vida*, chap. 5.

science; its study must be kept up, widened, supplemented, and enriched with reading, meditation, and observation all through life. Many find no interest in the study of spiritual facts and phenomena because they lack the necessary training. The purpose of an ascetical and mystical course is to supply such training and to arouse that kind of interest.

E. THE DISTINCTION BETWEEN ASCETICAL AND MYSTICAL THEOLOGY

11. "Ascetical" and "mystical" admit of a variety of uses. Each, when taken in a wide sense, includes the other. This means that when we speak of ascetical theology in a wide sense we speak of the study of Christian perfection in all its forms and manifestations, mystical contemplation and mystical phenomena not excluded. In a strict sense, however, ascetical theology is limited to the study of Christian perfection as it is commonly acquired under the influence of ordinary grace, infused contemplation and mystical phenomena not included. When, for many centuries, the study of Christian perfection was called mystical theology, the term "mystical" was taken in a broad sense to include also ascetical theology. For reasons of method, ascetical and mystical theology are treated separately by many authors of the present time, as explained above.

12. The question now arises whether, apart from this distinction in method, a real distinction exists between ascetical and mystical theology.

If the two terms are taken in a wide sense, no real distinction exists. If, however, they are taken in a strict sense, the question becomes controversial. At present there are two extremely opposed opinions on the subject, each opinion supported by a different school of thought. A. Poulain, S.J.,[10] followed by Bainvel, Marechal, Seisdedos, Reichstatter, Sharpe, Farges, De Guibert, and others, admits a real distinction between ascetical and mystical theology. R. Garrigou-Lagrange, O.P.,[11] followed by Arintero, Saudreau, Lamballe, Dom C. Butler, Dom Louismet, Tanquerey, Zahn, and others, denies such absolute distinction and insists that ascetical and mystical theology are one and continuous. There is the same difference of opinion regarding contemplation.[12] The reason seems clearer in the latter case because it is more specific. The question is whether acquired contemplation and infused contemplation are really and specifically distinct, or whether the distinction is merely one of degree. Poulain admits a specific distinction, Garrigou-Lagrange denies it and stands for a difference of degree only. Poulain has on his side the saints and mystical writers of the first order. They all affirm that infused contemplation and the mystical state which is so introduced cannot be acquired by any human effort or preparation. St. Theresa, speaking of this state, which she calls supernatural, says: "So I call that which no skill or effort of ours, however much we labor, can attain to." [13] Besides, the very terms, "infused" and "acquired" seem to imply such distinction and opposition. In acquired contemplation the soul is active and retains the initiative, whereas in infused contemplation the soul is passive, and the initiative remains with God

[10] *The Graces of Interior Prayer.*
[11] *Christian Perfection and Contemplation.*
[12] "On Acquired and Infused Contemplation," cf. Part II, chap. 7, nos. 160 ff.
[13] *Relationes espirituales*, rel. 5.

namely as to the time, place, and duration of the mystical prayer. Again, activity and passivity regarding the same action imply real distinction. The reason why Garrigou-Lagrange and his school deny a specific distinction is that his method is speculative. Acording to this method, as we have seen, theological principles must explain facts and phenomena. In our case the infused virtues and especially the gifts of the Holy Ghost can explain the higher facts of the spiritual life as they manifest themselves in an extraordinary and superhuman way. The explanation is beautiful, but we can hardly reconcile it with the actual experience of the mystics and with their description of the phenomena. It seems that we have here an attempt to force the facts to fit principles, or to draw conclusions not corroborated by facts.

13. We consider both opinions extreme. There is truth in each of them deserving of great attention, but we doubt that a clear and convincing solution can be given by either school, as long as they remain extreme. We suggest a combined method. We will consider facts and phenomena with A. Poulain, and theological principles with Garrigou-Lagrange, and we shall see that there is both a distinction and a continuity between acquired and infused contemplation, between asceticism and mysticism.

14. The distinction is not a specific one; this would be an essential distinction, a distinction *quoad rem,* which implies a different nature in acquired and infused contemplation, in ascetical and mystical. We simply deny such specific and essential difference, or difference *quoad rem,* and maintain a difference *quoad modum.* The essence of the thing itself is identical; in fact, the definition of contemplation is generically the same in both cases,

namely, "simple intellectual view of truth (*intuitus sim-plex veritatis*) higher than reason and accompanied by admiration." [14] The difference in acquired contemplation consists in assigning the manner or the means by which it is obtained, "which is the fruit of personal activity and diligence aided by grace." This same generic definition applies to infused contemplation, plus the difference of the manner or the *modus* by which it is obtained, "which is not the fruit of our activity as aided by grace, but of a special divine illumination." The value of the ten dollars a man has in his pocket is not specifically different, whether he has earned them by his own work or whether he has received them as a present from a friend. The difference is merely accidental and exterior, a difference *quoad modum* and not *quoad rem*.[15] In the second case the gift may be the cause of greater joy and satisfaction and similar accidental effects, but it will not change the essence of the thing itself, the amount of money. The very soul of spiritual life, whether ascetical or mystical, is the love of God, the *caritas Dei*, the sanctifying grace with infused virtues and gifts of the Holy Ghost. Nobody will admit for a moment that, in passing from the ascetical to the mystical state, a specific or essential change takes place in these divine elements of spiritual life. That loving knowledge of God, which is the substance of acquired contemplation, is not changed essentially when it becomes mystical and infused. Therefore we do not admit a specific distinction between ascetical theology and mystical theology, but we stand for an essential unity and

[14] St. Thomas, *Summa theol.*, IIa IIae, q. 180.
[15] Very illuminating in this respect is what St. Theresa writes in *Morada* IV, chapter 2 of her work *Las Moradas* (*The Mansions*).

continuity. Nor are we satisfied with the view of the other school, which in defending unity and continuity allows a simple difference of degree. As we have already shown in the present paragraph, a difference exists regarding the manner, or *modus,* and this is something else, and something more, than mere degree.

15. One may object that with this interpretation the mystical life would become something out of the ordinary way of sanctification, something exceptional. To this we reply that mystical life, taken in a wide sense of the term, is entirely within the ordinary way of sanctification. In a strict sense, however, it may be still the ordinary way of sanctification, but, being dependent on so many other conditions and circumstances, it actually remains or seems extraordinary and exceptional. Nor is there any reason to affirm that the good Lord must distribute His graces according to fixed rules.

CHAPTER II

THE CHRISTIAN LIFE

16. The proper object of ascetics is Christian perfection. More explicitly, it is the perfection of Christian life, because we consider Christian ascetical teaching in action and in its results rather than in theory only. Therefore we must determine the nature of Christian life itself before speaking of its perfection.

17. We learn the true concept of Christian life from Catholic dogma and moral. This is the foundation on which Christian perfection stands. Dogmatic or moral errors offer a defective basis incapable of supporting the lofty structure of Christian perfection. True asceticism and mysticism are found only where dogmatic and moral teaching is sound, in the Catholic Church. One of the most fundamental and far-reaching dogmas in the Christian religion is that of man's elevation to the supernatural order. Man was originally constituted in sanctity and justice.[1] This means that his human nature, created to the image of God, because of his spiritual and intellectual soul, was elevated to a much higher destiny through the infusion of sanctifying grace, a destiny entirely beyond and above the reach of all human power and human merit unaided by grace. The grace of God thus gave to His human image a divine likeness. This was the eternal plan of divine providence, a plan solemnly revealed in the

[1] Gen., chap. 3; Council of Trent, Sess. V.

act of man's creation: "Let us make man to our image and likeness." [2]

18. Original sin did not nullify man's elevation to the supernatural order, because of our divine Redeemer; but grace was lost and the divine likeness in man's soul was dimmed. He remained an image of God according to his nature and the natural order, but in the supernatural order that image did not resemble God any longer. Man became an image that had lost all its likeness. The divine light was extinguished in his eyes because the divine spark was gone from his soul. In the eyes of God man became a strange creature; God did not recognize His image in man any more. When man, the masterpiece of creation, made his first appearance on earth, all creatures felt that God was in him and they feared and obeyed him, who was made to the image and likeness of God. But all creatures became either indifferent or hostile to man the day he lost God's grace and resemblance; he became a strange creature to them also. No longer a king but a servant of sin,[3] the child of wrath [4] under the power of the devil and death, man discovered that this earth was no longer a paradise, no longer his home, but a place of exile, a valley of tears. His human nature, it is true, was not changed through sin; but it was stripped of all the supernatural and preternatural gifts and somewhat wounded and bruised in the soul's faculties. His mind was still there, and so were his will and his freedom, which he had so fearfully and so fatally abused.

19. But he found that his mind was hedged in by

[2] Gen. 1:26.
[3] Rom. 6:20.
[4] Eph. 2:3.

ignorance and threatened by error; concupiscence and fear made the choice between good and evil often difficult. Nature had not been changed; man was still destined for a supernatural order, but he was deprived of all the means of attaining it. The supernatural order consists essentially in the beatific vision and the possession of God in heaven. Man is by nature not equipped for such a goal; something divine must be added to his nature, a Godlike principle of life must be grafted on to his natural life and so make it able to perform Godlike, supernatural actions. Through these actions performed here on earth, he will merit a supernatural reward after death. It was God's goodness that elevated man to a supernatural order; it was God's infinite mercy that restored to man the necessary grace to attain his supernatural goal after he had lost it through sin. In this act of mercy a satisfaction to divine justice was offered by the sacrifice of the God-man. He came not only to satisfy divine justice for our sins, but also to teach us by word and especially by His example the path of virtue and perfection. He is the divine model for all those who strive after Christian perfection.

20. Human nature was created by God and it was found to be "very good," like all other created things.[5] The natural, essential goodness of human nature was not destroyed by original sin. False asceticism was one of the earliest heretical manifestations condemned by the Church because it was based on the assumption that matter, and consequently our body, is evil. Such were the Encratites (the "self-controlled") at the end of the first century. Of this sect St. Irenaeus writes: "Arising from Saturninus and Marcion, those who are called Encratites

[5] Gen. 1:31.

preached against marriage, thus setting aside the creation of God from the beginning, and indirectly blaming Him who made the male and the female for the propagation of the human race. Some of those that are among them have also introduced abstinence from meat, thus proving themselves ungrateful to God, who made all things." [6] The same heretical opinion was held by the Gnostics during the first three centuries of Christianity. According to them, all matter was a corruption of the divine; existence itself was an evil to be overcome by knowledge (gnosis). The Manichaeans of the third century went a step further, admitting a metaphysical and religious dualism, the existence of two eternal principles: God the principle of all good, and matter the cause of all evil. According to them the human body was the work of the supreme evil principle; its propagation through marriage was a crime. Similar ideas and principles were held by Albigensians and Catharists of the twelfth and thirteenth centuries. All flesh is in itself evil, they said; all spirit good. They even went so far as to encourage suicide.

Martin Luther considered human nature radically corrupted by original sin, so that justification by grace was something merely extrinsic, by imputation only, nature itself remaining hopelessly corrupted as before. This opinion is not only pessimistic but heretical. The opposite extreme is to be found in Pelagianism, which is over-optimistic regarding the goodness of human nature. It denied the existence of original sin and the necessity of divine grace, making human nature self-sufficient for salvation. This doctrine was condemned as heretical in 416. Between these two extremes we find the Catholic

[6] *Adver. haer,* I, 28.

doctrine of the true condition of human nature after its Fall and of the necessity of divine grace for salvation and sanctification.

21. In the plan of divine providence, human nature was to be aided and assisted by the sublime gifts of the preternatural and supernatural order. When these were lost, even though human nature was not essentially changed, its condition was worsened with respect to both body and soul.[7] Although the supernatural graces were fully restored to man through Christ, the preternatural gifts of integrity or immunity from inordinate concupiscence and from ignorance, and the gifts of impassibility and immortality were not restored. The way of life became steep and narrow. The life of the just became a ceaseless struggle against internal and external obstacles in the effort to subject his lower nature to his reason and his reason to God. After original sin, man's nature remains essentially good but contains much that is unruly and must be mortified, much that is imperfect and must be perfected. Nature must not be destroyed but be transformed, perfected. This, then, is the work of divine grace, and this is exactly the principle of St. Thomas: "Grace perfects nature and does not destroy it." [8]

22. Divine grace is a "participation in the divine nature." [9] Through grace we actually become "partakers of the divine nature." [10] Consequently we participate really and formally in the life and in the work of God, because nature is the ultimate principle of life and operation. Through grace we are reborn to a new life, we are "born

[7] Council of Trent, Sess. V, chap. 1.
[8] *Summa theol.*, Ia, q.1, a.8 ad2.
[9] *Ibid.*, Ia IIae, q.110, a.3.
[10] II Pet. 1:4.

of God," [11] and we become God's adoptive children and coheirs with Christ: "You have received the spirit of adoption of sons whereby we cry, Abba, Father." [12]

23. This is the supernatural life to which our human nature is elevated. As in natural life we distinguish a remote and a proximate principle of operation—the first being nature itself, the second our various faculties—so in supernatural life grace itself is the remote principle, and the infused virtues and gifts are the proximate principle of supernatural operation. Early in spiritual life we act more according to infused virtues; later on, especially when we have reached the unitive way, we act more under the guidance and inspiration of the Holy Ghost, in a more superhuman way, in virtue of the infused gifts.

In ascetical theology the entire treatise *De gratia* must be presupposed; the few notions about grace that have been reviewed here have the purpose of demonstrating the difference and the relation between the natural and the supernatural in the life of a Christian.

24. We owe this supernatural life to the Savior of mankind. With the parable of the good shepherd He has told us of His tender care for His sheep, that He came into this world "that they may have life, and may have it more abundantly." [13] The life of grace and the life of glory are meant here, since man already enjoyed the natural life. St. John Chrysostom, commenting on the Greek text of this passage, says: " 'I am come that they might have life, and that they might have more.' [14] And what is 'more' than life? The kingdom of heaven. But He does not as yet

[11] John 1:13.
[12] Rom. 8:15.
[13] John 10:10.
[14] Περισσὸν ἔχωσι.

say so, but dwells on the name of 'life,' which was known to them." [15]

25. Christian life here on earth is nothing but man's natural life purged of sin, original and individual, aided, perfected, and elevated by divine grace, and destined to a supernatural end. Christian life does not mean the death of our natural aspirations. Grace does not take the place of nature, as if nature did not exist any longer. This would be exaggerated supernaturalism, leading to all the follies of false mysticism. [16]

26. Instead of eliminating what is naturally good in the "natural," we must elevate it to the supernatural and sanctify it, otherwise life itself will become an impossibility and a crime, and we are right back among the old heresies of the Manichaeans and Albigensians. Of our blessed Savior, Isaias said: "The bruised reed he shall not break, and smoking flax he shall not quench." [17] Our poor fallen nature was the bruised reed. Our Lord was careful not to break it, but offered it the support of His grace that it might acquire new life, grow strong, and be more than itself again.

27. It is a doctrine condemned by the Church many times in the past, that whatever man does without the assistance of divine grace, or without referring the action to the supernatural end, is a sin. Martin Luther asserted that, after the Fall, man's free will exists only as a mere title, and therefore man sins grievously even while doing the best that he can according to his nature. This doctrine is contained in the thirty-sixth of his condemned proposi-

[15] *Hom.* 59 *in Ioan.*
[16] See encyclical letter of Pope Pius XII, *Mystici Corporis,* issued June 29, 1943, condemning false mysticism.
[17] Isa. 42:3.

tions.[18] It was condemned with the others by Pope Leo X in 1520.

Michael du Bay asserted that our free will, without the help of divine grace, can do nothing but sin, and therefore all the actions of the infidels are sinful and the virtues of philosophers are nothing but vices. These errors were condemned by Pope St. Pius V in 1567.[19] Similar errors were repeated by the Jansenists, who held that it is a necessity for the infidel to sin in whatever he does; they were condemned by Alexander VIII in 1690.[20] Shortly after this condemnation, Quesnel repeated more or less the same error and was condemned by Clement XI in 1713.[21]

If we cannot say that an infidel, without the help of divine grace, commits sin in whatever he does, how much less can we say that of the faithful Christian in the state of sanctifying grace, when he seeks an innocent natural relaxation, such as taking a walk or playing the piano, without referring it to the supernatural end? Such a man may give alms out of natural pity for the unfortunate; should we call such action a sin? Certainly not.

28. We are not advocating any neglect of a supernatural intention in whatever we do, nor are we unaware of St. Paul's advice: "All whatsoever you do in word or in work, do all in the name of the Lord Jesus Christ, giving thanks to God and the Father by Him." [22] This is the ideal Christian practice and it implies some degree of Christian perfection. But we are set against the method

[18] Denz., 776.
[19] *Ibid.*, 1025, 1027.
[20] *Ibid.*, 1298.
[21] *Ibid.*, 1351 f.
[22] Col. 3:17.

of calling sinful everything that is not perfect. There is a great deal of goodness between perfection and imperfection. A wrong conscience has never been a dependable guide to perfection, and a conscience based on principles of exaggerated and misinterpreted supernaturalism cannot be called right.

29. There are actions that are naturally good without being supernatural, and such actions can be performed even by infidels: "The Gentiles, who have no law, do by nature those things that are of the law, these having not the law, are a law to themselves." [23] "There is a love that is divine [i.e., supernatural] and another that is human [purely natural]; human love may be licit or illicit. . . . Licit is the human love with which a man loves his own wife, illicit that love with which a harlot or another man's wife is loved. . . . You ought to have this kind of licit love: it is merely human, but as I said, it is licit. And it is not only licit in the sense that it may be permitted, but so that its absence is considered reprehensible. You are allowed to love with human love your own wives, your children, your friends, your fellow citizens. . . . But you understand that this kind of love can be found even among sinners, pagans, Jews, heretics." [24] Here, according to St. Augustine, we have purely human actions, of a most common occurrence and a most profound nature, which are not only lawful but so essential to our life that their absence would be considered reprehensible in both saints and sinners. "However, that we may not seem to be contentious, let us grant that there are people that live right among the pagans." [25]

[23] Rom. 2:14.
[24] St. Augustine, *Serm.* 349, 1, 2.
[25] St. Chrysost., *Hom.* 28 *in Ioan.*

30. According to Sacred Scripture and the Fathers, therefore, there are human actions that are naturally good, although not deserving of a supernatural reward. Such actions are not to be called imperfections or sins. But a Christian who neglects to elevate such actions to the supernatural order misses the opportunity of acquiring supernatural merits through them. If this may be called imperfection on his part, the nature of those actions is not changed by his neglect. While stressing the necessity of the supernatural, we should not forget that nature was God's first revelation to man, and that all of it is one stupendous work written by God and telling man of God's wisdom, power, goodness, beauty, and glory. In saints like St. Francis of Assisi nature and grace were wed in a most happy union. A wonderful harmony resulted from the fact that they had learned to avoid and to check all that is unruly and discordant in nature, a harmony reminiscent of the happy days of the Garden of Eden before the Fall. If we strive to harmonize all that is good and beautiful in our human nature and in nature around us with divine grace and the supernatural order, the way of Christian perfection will be easier and safer. It will be freed from the gloom that Jansenists and false rigorists of all ages have cast upon it. Asceticism does not mean joylessness, and true virtue has nothing to do with sadness and gloom. The life of a good Christian, no matter what his vocation may be, is service to God. Gladness must be written on the countenance of God's servants, whether angels or men: "Sing joyfully to God, all the earth: serve ye the Lord with gladness." [26]

[26] Ps. 99:1.

CHAPTER III

NATURE OF CHRISTIAN PERFECTION

The Concept of Perfection

31. The word "perfection" is a substantive expressing, first of all, the completeness of an action (from *perficere*), then the resulting superior excellence or quality of a thing that has been subjected to such a thorough action. A thing or person is called perfect when it lacks none of the qualities required by its own nature. The word "perfect" is taken in its proper and literal sense when we say someone is a perfect gentleman; it is employed in a figurative sense when we say he is a perfect liar. Perfection, as the term is commonly used, implies always some superior quality or the excellence of good qualities.

32. According to St. Thomas [1] we may consider perfection in nature, in grace, and in glory. The perfection of nature appeared in all its beauty on the seventh day of creation when the divine work was complete and sin had not yet impaired nature's integrity. The perfection of grace was revealed in Christ's Incarnation, and the perfection of glory will be manifested at the end of the world. We are concerned here not with absolute but with relative perfection, the perfection of a Christian who is still a wayfarer here on earth. Nature and grace are elements and efficient causes of this perfection. In the preceding chapter we touched upon the relative goodness

---

[1] *Summa theol.*, Ia, q. 73, a. 1 ad 1.

of human nature, and we have seen how its integrity or perfection was lost through sin and how it can be regained through grace. As to the perfection of divine grace, we need merely point out that it partakes of the divine nature, and therefore is absolutely perfect. Its presence in our souls, even though it frees us from sin and makes us just and pleasing to God, does not make us perfect Christians. Perfection depends both on the help of grace and on the cooperation of nature. Grace respects our free will and demands its cooperation in the sublime work of making us like the divine ideal. Any Christian who reaches his heavenly home must be called perfect, because, as St. Thomas says, "a thing is said to be perfect in so far as it attains to its proper end, which is the ultimate perfection thereof." [2] The object of our study is Christian perfection not in its end (*in termino*) but in the way (*in via*), hence a perfection that is only relative and progressive. Having so defined our scope, we may ask: In what does Christian perfection consist?

Various Opinions

33. Socrates seems to have identified man's perfection with the virtue of justice. He teaches that the just man and the happy are one and the same.[3] Plato, as Clement of Alexandria remarks,[4] places perfection in the knowledge of the Good and in being like God, this likeness being justice and holiness with wisdom. Clement, as a loyal Platonist, accepts Plato's opinion after Christianizing it.

Some early Christian ascetics of the Orient thought that

---

[2] IIa IIae, q. 184, a. 1.
[3] Clem. Alex., *Strom.*, II, 22.
[4] *Ibid.*

perfection consists in external acts of penance and corporal austerities, an opinion rejected by Cassian [5] and
others. St. Jerome considers voluntary poverty and detachment from all created things as the crown of perfection: "The crown of perfect and apostolic virtue is to
sell all that one has and to distribute to the poor, and thus
freed from all earthly encumbrance to rise towards
Christ." [6] Several Eastern spiritual writers, including
Macarius the Egyptian, St. Nilus, Cassian, and St. John
Climacus, have given a Christian meaning to the Stoic
apatheia, defining Christian perfection as a state of complete and perfect control over passions and emotions. "I
consider the tranquillity of mind or *apatheia* to be nothing else but the heaven of the mind in our heart. . . . This
perfection of all perfect ones, this infinite perfection, as
I was told by one who has experienced it, so sanctifies
our mind, abstracting it from material things, that for the
greater part of our mortal life . . . the same mind is lifted
up by rapture to divine contemplation." [7] According
to St. Jerome,[8] Evagrius of Pontus wrote a book, Περὶ
ἀπαθείας, now lost, which was widely circulated among
the monks of the East. The Pelagians, too, considerered
perfection the mastery over one's passions, acquired by
human will-power unaided by grace, the process of becoming "as insensible as a stone and as impassible as God
Himself."

In the course of time perfection has been identified with
one or another moral virtue. Some found it in the virtue
of patience and endurance, basing their opinion on the

[5] *Collatio*, I, 7.
[6] *Ep.* 130, *ad Demetriadem*, 14.
[7] *Scala paradisi*, 29.
[8] *Adv. Pelag., Prolog.*

words of St. James: "Patience hath a perfect work." [9]
Others found it to reside in the multitude of prayers and
variety of devotions to which they were faithful. St.
Jerome reports such people existed in his day in Syria,
and were known as Euchites or Massalians ("the praying
ones").[10]

Under the false appearance of mysticism, theosophists,
like pantheists, make man's perfection reside in a certain
consciousness of his identity with God. Theosophism,
which resolves itself in atheism, is a deceptive imitation
and a perversion of Christian asceticism and mysticism.

Thesis: *Christian perfection in this life consists essentially in charity.*

EXPLANATION OF TERMS

34. Perfection is taken here to mean superior quality
or excellence of Christian living produced by the har-
monious and generous cooperation of human nature with
divine grace. It is a perfection that is only relative; it can
coexist with imperfections and light venial sins. But it is
progressive, never attaining in this life a degree that can
be considered supreme or absolute. Charity means here
primarily the love of God and secondarily the love of our
neighbor. This love is supernatural both in its object and
in its motive. Sensible emotions do not pertain to the act
of charity, and their absence is no indication of imperfect
charity.

The thesis expresses the common opinion prevailing in
the Church with regard to the nature of Christian perfec-

[9] Jas. 1:4.
[10] St. Jerome, *Adv. Pelag., Prol.*

tion. It is the doctrine of St. Thomas [11] and of all theologians after him.

35. Proofs from Sacred Scripture and from theological reasons.

1) "Above all these things have charity, which is the bond of perfection." [12]

2) Christian perfection consists in that bond by which man is united to God, his supreme end. Man is united to God by the bond of charity. Therefore Christian perfection consists in charity.

The major proposition is evident from the words of St. Thomas: "A thing is said to be perfect in so far as it attains its proper end, which is its ultimate perfection." [13] If a virtue is responsible for the attainment of the supreme end, that virtue constitutes the essence of perfection.

The minor is demonstrated from Scripture: (a) When our Lord was asked by a certain lawyer what one must do to possess eternal life (i.e., the supreme end, God Himself), He answered by confirming the lawyer's words: "Thou shalt love the Lord thy God with thy whole heart and with thy whole soul, and with all thy strength, and with all thy mind: and thy neighbor as thyself . . . this do, and thou shalt live." [14] (b) "God is charity: and he that abideth in charity, abideth in God, and God in him." [15] (c) "If any one love Me, he will keep My word, and my Father will love him, and We will come to him, and will make Our abode with him." [16]

3) Hence perfection consists in that virtue which em-

[11] IIa IIae, q. 184, a. 1.
[12] Col. 3:14.
[13] IIa IIae, q. 184, a. 1.
[14] Luke 10:25, 29.
[15] I John 4:16.
[16] John 14:23.

bodies all other virtues and all the precepts.[17] But only charity embodies all other virtues and all the precepts. Therefore perfection consists in charity.

The major is evident. The minor is demonstrated from Scripture: (a) Of the commandment of the love of God, Christ said: "This is the greatest and the first commandment. And the second is like to this: Thou shalt love thy neighbor as thyself. On these two commandments dependeth the whole law and the prophets." [18] (b) St. Paul tells the Romans that "love is the fulfilling of the law." [19] The same apostle, in the well-known thirteenth chapter of his First Epistle to the Corinthians, which has been rightly styled the canticle of love, teaches explicitly that all other virtues, gifts, and charismata are nothing without charity. Of charity itself he says that it basically contains all other virtues: "Charity is patient, is kind: charity envieth not, dealeth not perversely; is not puffed up; is not ambitious, seeketh not her own, is not provoked to anger, thinketh no evil; rejoiceth not in iniquity, but rejoiceth with the truth; beareth all things, believeth all things, hopeth all things, endureth all things. Charity never falleth away: whether prophecies shall be made void, or tongues shall cease, or knowledge shall be destroyed." [20]

4) The preceding argument may be presented from another point of view as follows: Christian perfection resides in that virtue the very nature of which implies

---

[17] Charity embodies all other virtues not by eliciting their respective acts but by commanding them: "Since charity has for its object the last end of human life, . . . it follows that it extends to the acts of a man's whole life, by commanding them, not by eliciting immediately all acts of virtue" (St. Thomas, IIa IIae, q.23, a.4).

[18] Matt. 22:38–40.

[19] Rom. 13:10.

[20] I Cor. 13:4–8.

God's friendship. Now this is true with charity alone, because all other virtues, including faith and hope, can exist without God's actual friendship. Therefore Christian perfection consists in charity.

5) Consensus of the Fathers.

36. (a) St. Augustine: "Perfect charity is perfect sanctity or justice." [21] "The love of God to the extent of despising self makes the heavenly city." [22] "My specific gravity is love; it takes whithersoever I am borne." [23]

b) St. John Chrysostom: "No matter what kind of good works one may have, they are all in vain if charity is not there." [24]

c) St. John Climacus: "Charity makes us like unto God, as far as it is possible for mortals to be so." [25]

d) St. Gregory the Great: "O how good is charity, which renders present to each other by virtue of love things that are far apart, which unites things that are divine, brings order among things that are confused, binds together things that are unequal, perfects what is imperfect! How right, then, was the excellent preacher in calling it the bond of perfection, because, while other virtues generate perfection, it is charity that binds them together so that they may never again escape from the loving mind!" [26]

37. Objections. (1) The act of the intellect is superior to the act of the will. Therefore perfection should consist in faith, which is an act of the intellect rather than in charity, which is an act of the will.

[21] *De natura et gratia,* 70, 84.
[22] *De Civ. Dei,* 14, 28.
[23] *Pondus meum amor meus: eo feror quocumque feror. Confes.,* 13, 9.
[24] *Hom. 8 in Ep. ad Col.*
[25] *Scala paradisi,* 30.
[26] *Ep. ad Virgil., Ep.* 5, 53.

Reply: With reference to created things, the knowledge of them is superior to the love of them. For example, the knowledge of the law of gravitation is superior to the love of it. The love of God, however, is superior to the knowledge of God: sinners and devils have a knowledge of God, but they do not love him, that is why their minds are ignoble and their condition wretched.

2) From the words of our Lord, "If thou wilt be perfect, go sell what thou hast, and give to the poor, and thou shalt have treasure in heaven: and come and follow Me," [27] it appears that perfection consist in voluntary poverty and in the following of Christ.

Reply: With those words, the Savior counsels evangelical perfection, indicating the fundamental conditions for the attainment of perfection; but he does not explain the nature of perfection itself.

3) In the enumeration of the beatitudes [28] no mention is made of charity, whereas the highest Christian perfection is described.

Reply: Charity is not explicitly mentioned but it is implicitly presupposed in each beatitude. Virtues and beatitudes, so far as they are an effect of charity, are in direct relation to perfection. "The perfection of the Christian life consists simply in charity, but in other virtues relatively." [29]

38. Cajetan and Suarez, commenting on the above-mentioned passages from the *Summa,* maintain that the relation of all other virtues to Christian perfection is an accidental one; in the work of perfection they are instru-

[27] Matt. 19:21.
[28] Matt. 5:3 ff.
[29] St. Thomas, *Summa theol.,* IIa IIae, q. 184, a. 1 ad 2.

ments and secondary means, whereas charity is the very essence of perfection, its very soul.

39. "God is love"; and for a Christian, love is everything. Our immortal soul, created to the image and likeness of God, is united to our body by necessity of nature, but to God by love. This turning of the soul to God is another proof of the soul's divine origin and of its being a living image of God: "The image of God is noted in the soul according as the soul turns to God, or possesses a nature that enables it to turn to God." [30] The soul's life in God is love. Anything that wounds or kills that love, wounds and kills that life. Christian perfection is the perfection of charity, and therefore the perfection of our life in God. According to the teaching of St. Augustine, the whole spiritual life of man and every advancement in perfection are based on charity: "Incipient charity is incipient justice; proficient charity is proficient justice; great charity is great justice; perfect charity is perfect justice." [31]

SCHOLIUM. PURE AND DISINTERESTED LOVE

40. Several errors about the nature of perfection and of love have been condemned by the Church in the past. Most of those errors were based on the false assumption that man can attain absolute perfection and impeccability in this life. The Beghards of the Middle Ages pretended "that man is able in the present life to attain to such a high degree of perfection that he becomes altogether impeccable and can no more grow in grace: because, as

[30] *Ibid.*, Ia, q.93, a.8.
[31] *De natura et gratia*, 70, 84.

they say, if anyone could advance always, he might become more perfect than Christ." [32]

Consistent with their false assumption of impeccability,
they affirmed that those who have reached such degree
of perfection need neither prayer nor mortification, and
can freely indulge in whatever they please; nor are they
bound by any obedience to civil or ecclesiastical authority, enjoying as they do the freedom of the Spirit. "It is
the duty of an imperfect man to practice virtue; a perfect
soul bids good-bye to virtues." And from here the Beghards go on to claim a still grosser license of the spirit, or
rather of the flesh.[33] These doctrines were condemned in
the Council of Vienne in 1312. Christian perfection remains always relative in this life; we must contend with
imperfections and venial sins owing to human frailty, no
matter how high we have risen in the perfection of charity.
Impeccability is a divine privilege; and we know that
it was granted to the Blessed Virgin Mary [34] because of
her singular position as Mother of God.

In spite of the condemnation of the Church, these
doctrines were revived by Molinos, who asserted that,
through acquired contemplation, one reaches the state
in which no sins are committed, either mortal or venial.[35]
His principles were put into practice and became the
source of many scandalous disorders. The Holy Office
condemned 68 of his propositions on November 20, 1687.
He and two hundred of his disciples were taken into
custody; after a confession of his immorality he was con-

[32] Denz., 471.
[33] *Ibid.*, 472–77.
[34] Council of Trent, Sess. VI, can. 23. The Blessed Virgin was impeccable,
not by the essential perfection of her nature, but by a special divine privilege.
[35] Denz., 1277.

demned to life imprisonment. He died nine years later, after abjuring his doctrines.

41. Another more subtle aberration regards the nature of love itself. "There is an habitual state of the love of God which is pure charity without admixture of any motive of self-interest. Neither the fear of punishments nor the desire of rewards has part in it any longer." This is the first of the twenty-three propositions of Archbishop François Fénelon, taken from his little book, *Explications des maximes des saints sur la vie intérieure* (Paris, 1697), and condemned by Innocent XII, March 12, 1699. According to Fénelon this kind of disinterested love goes so far that a person becomes indifferent to reprobation and damnation, and to the loss of all hope of salvation. In this case, he advises the spiritual director to allow such a soul to acquiesce in the loss of its eternal interest and in its just damnation.[36] This exaggerated and distorted notion of love is a negation of the very nature of love. The presence of some good is essential for love, because love is an act of the will, and the object of this act of the will is what is good. If that good is loved and desired because it is good for us, then we have the love that is called of concupiscence. When the good is loved for its own sake, we have the love of friendship, and charity is a friendship. According to St. Francis de Sales: "Friendship cannot be unless it be reciprocal, having for its basis communication, and for its end union. I speak so for the benefit of certain fantastic and empty spirits, who very often on mere imaginations nourish morbid thoughts to their own great affliction."[37]

[36] Propositions 9–12; Denz., 1335–38.
[37] *Treatise on the Love of God,* Book X, chap. 10.

42. God is our supreme end. Only a fool can be indifferent and disinterested with regard to his own supreme end. We cannot love God without implicitly loving our own supreme, eternal happiness, because He himself is our end, our "reward exceedingly great." Here, too, we cannot "put asunder what God has joined together." A perfect and pure love of God consists in loving God for His own sake; but His own sake is also our own good. To love God and remain indifferent to our own reprobation and damnation, is an absurdity, for a reprobate is an enemy of God, one who hates God and is hated by God. Hence this is not love at all.

43. The reciprocal love of God for the loving soul is mentioned often in Sacred Scripture: "I love them that love Me"; [38] "If anyone love Me, he will keep My word, and My Father will love him, and We will come to him and will make Our abode with him"; [39] "The Father Himself loveth you, because you have loved Me." [40]

That this love of God for us is a love of friendship is manifest also from the fact that Christ calls His faithful disciples His friends: "You are My friends, if you do the things that I command you"; [41] and in the following verse of the same chapter: "I will not now call you servants: for the servant knoweth not what his lord doth. But I have called you friends: because all things whatsoever I have heard of My Father, I have made known to you."

THE PERFECTION OF CHARITY

44. Thesis. In this life, the perfection of charity con-

[38] Prov. 8:17.
[39] John 14:23.
[40] John 16:27.
[41] John 15:14.

sists essentially in the observance of the commandments, secondarily and instrumentally in the observance of the counsels.[42]

We know that we are held to the observance of the commandments of God under pain of sin and eternal damnation. We know also that the Gospel contains counsels of Christian perfection: voluntary poverty, virginity, and perfect obedience to superiors. In the preceding thesis we affirmed that Christian perfection consists in charity. Does the present thesis contradict what we have affirmed there? Certainly not; it explains it. It was noted above that charity sums up all the commandments, the counsels, and the virtues. Since all people are bound to keep the commandments in order "to enter into life," it seems that perfection of charity should consist essentially in the observance of the counsels; hence the ordinary Christian, who has no desire for perfection, could be satisfied with keeping the commandments, while he who strives after perfection, like the religious, should keep the counsels. This would be an entirely erroneous idea of perfection and of charity. The essence of charity consists in doing the manifest will of God, even unto death. This will of God is clearly manifest in the commandments, because the commandments are for every person having the use of reason. The same is not true of the counsels. As a matter of fact, we are sure that God does not will that every person should observe the counsel of lifelong virginity. Nor can every person on earth, in the ordinary social order, renounce all ownership of property according to the accepted concept of evangelical poverty. Christian perfection was meant for all and not for a minority in the Church.

[42] Cf. St. Thomas, *Summa theol.*, IIa IIae, q.184, a.3.

Therefore it must consist in something that all can practice, whether rich or poor, married or single, and all persons can and must observe the commandments. The
commandments point out the ordinary part of charity and
perfection: "Perfection of charity is commanded to man
in this life, because a person does not run right unless he
knows whither to run. And how shall we know this if no
commandment declares it to us?" [43] Charity cannot exist
without the observance of the commandments, but it can
well exist without the keeping of the counsels. "The commandments, other than the precept of charity, are directed to the removal of things contrary to charity, that
is, things with which charity is incompatible, whereas
the counsels are directed to the removal of things that
hinder the act of charity, and yet are not contrary to
charity, such as marriage, the occupation of worldly business, and so forth." [44] These words of St. Thomas explain
the real place held by the counsels in the work of perfection: they remove those things that are not contrary to
charity but that hinder its perfect function; they make
the way of perfection safer and easier, and therefore they
contribute instrumentally to the perfection of charity.

45. Scriptural texts upon which our thesis is based.

1) "Thou shalt love the Lord thy God with thy whole
heart"; [45] and "Thou shalt love thy neighbor as thyself"; [46]
and these are the commandments of which our Lord said:
"On these two commandments dependeth the whole law
and the prophets." [47]

[43] St. Augustine, *De perf. justit.*, 8.
[44] St. Thomas, *loc. cit.*
[45] Deut. 6:5.
[46] Lev. 19:18.
[47] Matt. 22:40.

2) "He that hath My commandments and keepeth them, he it is that loveth Me." [48]

3) "If you keep My commandments, you shall abide in My love." [49]

4) "You are My friends, if you do the things that I command you." [50]

5) "The end of the commandment is charity, from a pure heart, and a good conscience, and an unfeigned faith." [51] The difference between commandment and counsel is briefly explained by St. Augustine thus: "The commandment is such that, if you do not obey it, you sin; but if you do not keep the counsel, you commit no sin, but you achieve a lesser good." [52]

[48] John 14:21.
[49] John 15:10.
[50] John 15:14.
[51] I Tim. 1:5.
[52] *De virginitate*, XV, 15.

CHAPTER IV

THE OBLIGATION OF TENDING TO PERFECTION

46. Thesis. The duty of tending to perfection is incumbent upon all Christians according to their vocation and state in life.

Perfection, in this life, is something relative and progressive; it admits of different degrees just as charity does and in the same proportion. Growth in charity is growth in perfection and sanctity. There is an initial or substantial perfection corresponding to the *caritas inchoata* of St. Augustine. This first degree of perfection consists in the avoidance of all mortal sins by keeping all the grave commandments. The second degree, or *caritas provecta,* consists in avoiding also venial sins that are fully deliberate, by keeping all the commandments even when they oblige under the pain of venial sin. The third degree, comprising both the *caritas magna* and the *caritas perfecta,* consists not only in the avoidance of all deliberate sins but also in the practice of virtues, of supererogatory good works, and especially in the keeping of the evangelical counsels.

47. The thesis regards all Christians individually, irrespective of their state in life. But the state in life may impose a second obligation to work for perfection, as in the case of religious, who live in the state of perfection. The state of perfection does not imply that they are perfect, but that the state of life they have embraced is such that, if they live in accordance with it, with the help of God, they will attain perfection, thanks to the evangelical counsels and the rule they observe. Canon law directly and indirectly speaks of this obligation as binding on religious; first in the definition it gives of the religious state as such; "A permanent manner of living in community wherein the faithful, in addition to those things that are of precept, engage themselves by vow to observe the evangelical counsels of obedience, chastity, and poverty"; [1] more explicitly in canon 593: "Each and every religious superior as well as subject is bound to tend toward the perfection of his state." A religious is obliged under pain of mortal sin, according to St. Alphonsus,[2] to tend to perfection. This obligation, however, is fulfilled through an ordinary observance of the rule and the keeping of the vows.

48. Priests, both regular and secular, are obliged to a higher perfection than that of the simple religious. Dionysius the Pseudo-Areopagite describes the various degrees of perfection of prelates and ministers of the Church as similar to those of the celestial hierarchy of the angels as follows: "The order of pontiffs is consummative and perfecting, that of the priests is illuminative and light-giving, that of the ministers is cleansing and discretive." [3] Here we have a foreshadowing of the "three ways" of spiritual life: the purgative, the illuminative, and the unitive way, each implying a different degree of perfection. Such a function and perfection regard more the exterior;

---

[1] Can. 487.
[2] *Theol. mor.*, IV, 18.
[3] *Eccl. hier.*, 5.

the perfection of the priest we have in mind here is the inward perfection. "From the fact that a man receives a sacred order he is not placed simply in the state of perfection, although inward perfection is required in order that one exercise such acts worthily." [4] "By holy orders a man is appointed to the most august ministry of serving Christ Himself in the sacrament of the altar. For this requires a greater inward holiness than that which is requisite for the religious state." [5] The Pseudo-Areopagite says that priests must set such an example of perfection as to be a model for religious.[6] The same idea was expressed by St. Isidore of Pelusium: "The priests must be holier and purer than those who went into the solitude of the mountains." [7] St. Jerome's letter to Nepotian, who had abandoned the military life for the priesthood and who was now (A.D. 394) a priest at Altinum, is really a treatise on the duties of the clergy in general and on priestly perfection in particular. A few quotations from this letter, which has enjoyed great vogue, will not be irrelevant.

A cleric, then, serving the Church of Christ, must first understand the meaning of his name; and then, when he realizes this, he must endeavor to be that which he is called. For since the Greek word "kleros" means "lot" or "inheritance," the clergy are so called either because they are the lot of the Lord, or else bcause the Lord Himself is their lot and portion. . . . Do not look to your military experience for a standard of clerical obligations. Under Christ's banner look not for worldly gain. . . . Welcome poor men and strangers to your homely board, that with them Christ may be your guest. . . . Always bear in mind that it was a woman who expelled the tiller of paradise from his heritage. . . . Beware of

---

[4] St. Thomas, IIa IIae, q. 184, a. 6.
[5] *Ibid.*, a. 8.
[6] *Eccl. hier.*, 6.
[7] *Epist. Palladio episc.; Lib. II, epist.* 284.

all that gives occasion for suspicion; and, to avoid scandal, shun every act that may give color to it. . . . It is the glory of a bishop to make provision for the wants of the poor; but it is the shame of priests if they amass private fortunes. . . . Do not let your deed belie your words; lest when you speak in church someone may mentally reply, "Why do you not practice what you profess? Here is a lover of dainties turned censor. His stomach is full, and he reads us a homily on fasting." . . . In a priest of Christ, mouth, mind, and hand should be at one.

St. John Chrysostom's work *De sacerdotio* in six books is the most eloquent treatise on the dignity, sanctity, and power of the priesthood. The many authoritative pronouncements of the Church on the subject of clerical perfection have been embodied in canon 124 of the Code of Canon Law: "Clerics must lead an interior and exterior life holier than that of the laity and give these the good example of virtue and good works."

49. The duty of tending to perfection is universal. No state of life, no individual person, has a monopoly on virtue, perfection, or heroic sanctity. Every state and every condition of life have given saints to the Church of God. The married, and the unmarried living in the world, like the religious men and women of the cloister, have given perfect souls and great saints to God. Kings and queens and the lowliest of subjects shine before God with the same crown of glory. The great luminaries of science and learning and the poor illiterate man and woman whose only schooling was whatever instruction they received in church have all acquired the one life-giving knowledge: the science of the saints. Men of business, military men, men and women of every profession, have become saints. To prove our assertion it will suffice to read through the *Martyrology*, the *Acta Sanctorum* of the Bollandists, or

any up-to-date *Book of Saints.* No doubt, the clerical and
the religious state can muster a larger number of saints
than the laity. It would be surprising if it were not so,
since the way of perfection and sanctity is made consid-
erably easier and safer for them.

50. "Tending to perfection" means taking sufficient
measures to preserve the supernatural life of grace in our
souls, first by protecting and defending it against all the
assaults of spiritual enemies (the world, the flesh, and the
devil), secondly by taking positive steps to strengthen
and to increase that same life by good works, by prayer,
by the practice of virtues, because to attack is to defend
oneself more vigorously. This kind of tending to perfection is essential since it regards the very life of our souls,
without which we cannot attain our supernatural end. To
some degree and to some extent, each of the faithful must
tend to perfection in this way in order to insure his eternal
salvation, After being sanctified by divine grace, we must
cooperate with it in a positive way that we may persevere
in the same state of grace. "The cooperation of our free
will with the divine help is needed not only that we may
become good and honest . . . but also that, after becoming good and honest, we may persevere in virtue." [8] As
St. Augustine teaches in his work *De correptione et gratia,*
there is a great deal of difference between *Posse non peccare* and *non posse peccare* ("being able not to sin," and
"not being able to sin"). The first was the condition of
the first man before his fall; the second, the happy condition of eternal perseverance in heaven. With the grace of
God, we, too, are able not to sin, but we must ask continually and beseechingly for such divine help. It is a dogma

[8] Origen, *Comm. in Ps.* 4.

of faith that the final perseverance, on which our eternal salvation depends, must be obtained by prayer and good works from God.[9] The warnings of St. Paul are directed to every one of the faithful: "He that thinketh himself to stand, let him take heed lest he fall"; [10] "With fear and trembling work out your salvation." [11] All this implies that to persevere we cannot remain idle in spiritual life. Whatever we do in this respect is an integral part of the fulfillment of our obligation of tending to perfection.

51. Perfection, as we have seen, is progressive, it tends always toward betterment, always toward a higher goal in virtue, in imitation of the divine ideal of sanctity. The evangelical counsels lift up the soul to a higher sphere of Christian perfection, to a closer following of Christ and His apostles. When we speak of Christian perfection in the proper sense of the word, it is this perfection which includes the keeping of the counsels either *in re* or in spirit.

52. The thesis expresses the common opinion of theologians. Sacred Scripture either explicitly or implicitly reminds us of our duty of tending to perfection. After proclaiming the eight beatitudes and the ideal of Christian perfection, our Lord concluded his Sermon on the Mount with the exhortation: "Be you therefore perfect, as also your heavenly Father is perfect." [12] These words were directed to each and every one of His hearers and not merely to His apostles; hence the duty of tending to perfection is universal.

The great commandment of loving God with our whole heart, and our neighbor as ourselves, implies a complete

[9] Denz., 132, 806, 832.
[10] I Cor. 10:12.
[11] Phil. 2:12.
[12] Matt. 5:48.

surrender of heart and mind to God, a surrender that
often requires great self-denial and supreme effort. This
commandment, as we have seen, is binding under pain
of losing God's friendship and being excluded from our
supernatural goal; the essence of Christian perfection
consists in this great commandment, as has been demonstrated above. Consequently everybody must tend to
perfection because everybody must keep the great
commandment of love.

The duty of the faithful to make serious efforts toward
perfection may be gathered from several expressions of
our Lord and His apostles, such as: "Strive to enter by the
narrow gate; for many, I say to you, shall seek to enter,
and shall not be able"; [13] "How narrow is the gate, and
strait is the way that leadeth to life; and few there are
that find it"; [14] "The kingdom of heaven suffereth violence, and the violent bear it away"; [15] "He that is just,
let him be justified still: and he that is holy, let him be
sanctified still"; [16] "He chose us in Him [Christ] before
the foundation of the world, that we should be holy and
unspotted in His sight in charity. Who hath predestinated
us unto the adoption of children through Jesus Christ
unto Himself: according to the purpose of His will"; [17]
"He gave some apostles, and some prophets, and other
some evangelists, and other some pastors and doctors, for
the perfecting of the saints, for the work of the ministry,
for the edifying of the body of Christ: until we all meet
into the unity of faith, and of the knowledge of the Son

[13] Luke 13:24.
[14] Matt. 7:14.
[15] Matt. 11:12.
[16] Apoc. 22:11.
[17] Eph. 1:4 f.

of God, unto a perfect man, unto the measure of the age
of the fulness of Christ. . . . Doing the truth in charity,
we may in all things grow up in Him who is the head, even
Christ"; [18] "Wherefore, brethren, labor the more, that by
goods works you may make sure your calling and election.
For doing these things, you shall not sin at any time." [19]

53. The Fathers of the Church are no less eloquent and
unanimous in exhorting the faithful to guarantee their
election and salvation by positive efforts, by the performance of good works: "A splendid and divine thing, dearest brethren, is the saving work of charity; a great comfort
of the faithful, a wholesome guard of our security, a pro-
tection of hope, a safeguard of faith, a remedy for sin, a
thing placed in the power of the doer, a thing both great
and easy, without the risk of persecution, a crown of
peace; the true and greatest gift of God, necessary for the
weak, glorious for the strong, assisted by which the Christian obtains spiritual grace, deserves well of Christ the
Judge, accounts God his debtor. For this palm of works
of salvation let us gladly and readily strive; let us all in
the struggle of righteousness, run with God and Christ
looking on; and let us who have already begun to be
greater than this life and the world, slacken our course by
no desire of this life and of this world." [20] "The love of
God is never idle. It performs great things when present." [21] "Love finds nothing hard; no task is difficult to the
eager. Think of all that Jacob bore for Rachel, the wife
who had been promised to him. Jacob, the Scripture says,
served seven years for Rachel. And they seemed to him

[18] Eph. 4:11–15.
[19] II Pet. 1:10.
[20] St. Cyprian, *De opere et eleem.*, 26.
[21] St. Gregory the Great, *Hom. in Ev.*, 30, 2.

but a few days for the love he had to her. . . . Unless you use force you will never receive the bread of life." [22] "The labors of those who love are not burdensome at all but they themselves are cause of delight. . . . In the thing that we love either we do not labor or we love the labor itself." [23] "The way of the present life pertains to those who advance, although those that advance well are called perfect wayfarers. The supreme perfection, however, to which nothing can be added, is that in which one begins to possess what he strives after." [24] "Forget the past; do not look back lest you remain there. Consider that we are wayfarers. You ask me: What is it to walk? I will tell you in one word: it is to advance, lest perhaps you may not understand and walk more lazily. Advance, my brethren; judge yourselves without deceit, without flattery, without wheedling, for there is nobody within you before whom you may blush or boast. There is one there who likes humility; let Him judge you, and you, too, be your own judge. If you want to arrive at that which you are not, you must dislike what you are, for wherein you please yourselves there you remain and when you have said: Enough! you have perished. Always add, always walk, advance always. Do not stand still on the road; do not turn back; do not leave the road. He who does not advance is standing still; he who turns to the things he has left is going backward; he who apostatizes wanders away from the road. A lame man on the road is better than a runner off the road." [25]

As a last proof of our thesis we add the following the-

[22] St. Jerome, *Epist.*, 22, 40.
[23] St. Augustine, *De bono vid.*, 21.
[24] St. Augustine, *De natura et gratia*, 12.
[25] St. Augustine, *Sermones*, 169.

ological reason. The perfection of charity consists essentially in the observance of the commandments, as already demonstrated in the preceding thesis. But everybody is obliged to observe the commandments. Therefore everybody is bound to tend to perfection.

THE IMITATION OF CHRIST

54. Whoever strives after perfection in any work of art must endeavor to imitate what is most beautiful and most perfect in his field. The model of Christian perfection is God Himself: "Be you therefore perfect as also your heavenly Father is perfect." [26] Nobody has seen the Father; it seems, therefore, that we are commanded to imitate the unseen and unknown. But seeing and knowing the Son, one sees and knows the Father: "Who seeth Me seeth the Father." [27] The Son of God, the God-man, is the ideal and the model proposed for our imitation: "For whom he foreknew, he also predestinated to be made conformable to the image of His Son; that He might be the firstborn amongst many brethren." [28] Christ's whole life was a sublime and divine example of virtue; His actions as well as His words are a revelation of divine wisdom. Christ Himself demands that we learn from Him: "Learn of Me, because I am meek and humble of heart: and you shall find rest to your souls." [29] On the eve of His death He could tell His disciples the reason of the great example of humility and love He had shown us: "I have given you an example, that as I have done to you, so do you also." [30]

[26] Matt. 5:48.
[27] John 14:9.
[28] Rom. 8:29.
[29] Matt. 11:29.
[30] John 13:13.

One of the most common exhortations of St. Paul is to imitate Christ: "I beseech you, be ye followers of me, as I also am of Christ"; [31] "Be ye therefore followers of God, as most dear children; and walk in love, as Christ also hath loved us, and hath delivered Himself for us." [32]

Christ, therefore, is the model of Christian perfection. The keeping of the commandments and the evangelical counsels, the observance of the great commandment of love, must tend to make us "conformable to the image" of the Son of God.

55. "Christ has given you power to become similar unto Him to the best of your ability. Fear not when you hear this. On the contrary, you should fear lest you become not like unto Him. Speak, therefore, as He did, and in this you will be similar unto Him, as far as man can be." [33] "If we, therefore, long for union with Him, we must contemplate His most divine life in the flesh and, by imitating His holy sinlessness, we must ascend to a state that is immaculate and godlike." [34]

"Every action, O dearest one, every word of our Savior Jesus Christ, is a pattern of virtue and piety. Wherefore, having shown us virtue and piety as in a picture, He also assumed our human nature, in order that every one of us, looking at it, might imitate his prototype and model according to his ability." [35] Pseudo-Macarius represents Christ as a sculptor always working at the heavenly image in us. He will succeed in His work only inasmuch as we keep our eyes fixed on Him all the time; if we turn

---

[31] I Cor. 4:16.
[32] Eph. 5:1 f.
[33] St. Chrysost., *Hom. in Matt.*, 78.
[34] Pseudo-Dionys., *Eccles. hier.*, III, 12.
[35] St. Basil, *Const. Asc.*, 1.

our back on Him and look at the things of this world, the
celestial image cannot be finished.[36]

Clement of Alexandria places the perfection of the true
Gnostic (the perfect Christian) in the imitation of God:
"He is the Gnostic who is after the image and likeness of
God, who imitates God as far as possible, deficient in
none of the things which contribute to the likeness as far
as compatible, practicing self-restraint and endurance,
living righteously, reigning over the passions, bestowing
what he has as far as possible, and doing good both by
word and by deed." [37]

On this subject of the imitation of Christ, the Fathers
of the Church are inexhaustible. St. Augustine, St. Maximus the Confessor, and many others regard this imitation
and assimilation as one of the motives for the Incarnation.
Imitation is one of the glorious effects of love. Love either
finds equals or it makes them such. Hence we understand
why of all virtues charity is the bond of perfection, because it tends by its very nature to render us similar to
God. Love had the same effect on God Himself: He assumed our human nature in order to be like unto man,
whom He loved; He made man partake of His divine nature by giving him His sanctifying grace. Such effects of
love were recognized even by great pagan minds like the
philosopher Plato.[38] "What conduct, then, is dear and
conformable to God? That which is characterized by one
word of old date: Like will be dear to like, as to what is
in proportion; but things out of proportion are dear

[36] Pseudo-Macarius, *Hom.* 30.
[37] *Stromata*, 19.
[38] Plato, *The Laws*.

neither to one another nor to those which are in proportion. And that, therefore, he that would be dear to God, must, to the best of his power, become such as He is." [39]

[39] Clement of Alexandria, *Stromata*, 22.

CHAPTER V

THE MOST COMMON MEANS OF CHRISTIAN PERFECTION

56. The means of attaining perfection are commonly divided into two classes: general means and special means. The former are more or less common to all degrees or stages of Christian perfection; the latter are peculiar to one particular stage or another. At present we shall treat of the general means only; in the second part of this book, in which the three ways are discussed, the special means will be explained.

The general means considered here are: prayer, the desire for perfection, knowledge of God and self, spiritual readings and instructions, spiritual direction, and a rule of conduct. The first three means are interior, the last three are exterior.

Some authors add the conformity to the divine will to the interior means of perfection. We consider conformity to the divine will one of the fruits of perfection itself; perfect conformity is perfect sanctity. It is the result of all our efforts sustained by grace.

Other general means of perfection not mentioned here are the frequent and devout reception of the sacraments of penance and the Eucharist, and attendance at or the celebration of Mass. Since ample exposition of these is given in moral and dogmatic theology, we shall not discuss them here.

A. Prayer

57. Prayer is the most universal means of salvation and sanctification. This is especially true of prayer of petition, which is ordinarily a vocal prayer. Mental prayer, on the contrary, is a particular and specific means of perfection. In fact, we distinguish the various degrees of ascetical and mystical life by the corresponding form and degree of mental prayer; for example, ordinary discursive prayer or meditation marks the purgative way, affective prayer the illuminative way, acquired contemplation the unitive way, and infused contemplation the mystical ways.

The efficacy of prayer as a general means of perfection is based on the divine promise: "Ask and you shall receive, seek and you shall find, knock and it shall be opened unto you." [1] Although many benefits in the natural and supernatural order are bestowed upon us through divine liberality without our asking for them, there are others, vital ones, which are granted only in answer to our prayer or at least through the prayer of the Church. This is what St. Alphonsus means when, like many doctors of the Church, he says that without prayer there is no salvation and, a fortiori, no perfection.

"Pray one for another, that you may be saved," says St. James (5:6). And St. Thomas says: "God grants many things to us out of His liberality, even without our asking for them: but that He wishes to grant us certain things at our asking, is for our own good, namely, that we may acquire confidence in having recourse to God, and that we may recognize in Him the author of our goods." [2]

[1] Matt. 7:7.
[2] IIa IIae, q. 83, a. 2 ad 3.

58. St. Basil (Hom. 5) defines the prayer of petition as "the asking of good things from God by pious persons." Though it is not necessary that it be expressed in words, since our pious desires, holy resolutions, and good deeds are often a prayer of this kind before God, nevertheless a prayer of petition is commonly a vocal prayer. St. Nilus calls prayer: "A conversing of the mind with God." [3] St. Jerome, speaking of both prayer and spiritual reading, says: "When you pray, you talk to your [divine] bridegroom; when you read, He talks to you." [4] St. John Climacus points out in a beautiful and comprehensive way the marvelous effects of prayer on the spiritual life:

Prayer, according to its nature, is a conversation and union between man and God; according to its efficacy, it is the very conservation of the world, our reconciliation with God, both the mother and the daughter of tears, a propitiation for sins, a bridge over temptations, a fortress against afflictions, the extinction of wars, the work of the angels, the nourishment of all spiritual substances, our future happiness, our eternal occupation, the source of virtues, the guardian of graces, spiritual advancement, the food of the soul, the illumination of the mind, the axe against despair, the evidence of hope, the dispelling of sadness, the riches of monks, the treasure of hermits, the diminution of anger, the mirror of our progress, the index of dimensions, the revelation of our own condition, a sign of things to come, a token of our future glory. [5]

To be effective, every prayer, vocal or mental, must come from the heart; it must be a cry of the soul. "The true petition does not consist in the voices of the mouth but in the thoughts of the heart. It is not our words but our

[3] *De oratione*, 3.
[4] *Epist.*, 22, 25.
[5] *Scala paradisi*, 28.

desires that make our voices stronger in God's most secret ears." [6]

"The cry of our heart," says St. Ambrose, "is not in the sound of the body but in the sublimity of our thoughts and the harmony of virtues. Great is the cry of faith. . . . Great is the voice of justice, great the voice of chastity whereby even the dead speak; not only do they speak but they cry out like Abel." [7]

59. Prayer, of all the above-mentioned general means of perfection, is the one expressly commanded by the Gospels.[8] The nature and extent of the necessity of prayer are treated in moral theology. For our purpose it is sufficient to note that anyone who wishes to advance in spiritual perfection must become first and above everything else a man of prayer. No other means at our disposal can take the place of prayer in the process of sanctification except the grace of God; and grace often depends upon our prayer. Mental prayer in all its forms and degrees will be treated in the second part of this volume and in mystical theology.

B. The Desire for Perfection

60. The desire for Christian perfection is an act of the human will, which, under the influence of divine grace, is working sincerely and effectively toward spiritual progress. Mere wishing can never accomplish anything; there must be an actual impulse of the soul toward perfection, a driving force that sets everything in motion and will

[6] St. Gregory the Great, *Moral.*, XXII, 17, 43.
[7] *Expos. in Ps.* 118.
[8] E.g., Matt. 7:7; Luke 11:9 f.; Matt. 26:41.

persevere undiminished in spite of opposition and handi-
caps. This very desire is a grace of God, but we may pray
for it and acquire the necessary disposition by avoiding
sin and its occasions. In the Book of Wisdom (7:7), we
read: "I wished, and understanding was given me: and
I called upon God, and the spirit of wisdom came upon
me." The love of desire (because desire is love of a good
that is absent) for perfection is produced in us by the
Spirit of understanding and especially by the Spirit of
wisdom. It will come upon us if we call upon God and if
our hearts are free from sordid affections. This desire for
perfection is God's wisdom in us, because we have come
to appraise things according to their true value. It is a
most precious gift and should be highly esteemed: "And
I preferred her [this divine wisdom] before kingdoms
and thrones, and esteemed riches nothing in comparison
of her. Neither did I compare unto her any precious stone:
for all gold in comparison of her, is as a little sand, and sil-
ver in respect to her shall be counted as clay. I loved her
above health and beauty, and chose to have her instead
of light: for her light cannot be put out. Now all good
things came to me together with her, and innumerable
riches through her hands, and I rejoiced in all these: for
this wisdom went before me, and I knew not that she was
the mother of them all." [9]

"It is very important," says St. Theresa, "not to stifle
our desires. On the contrary, we must believe that with
divine help and our own efforts we, too, can in the course
of time obtain what so many saints, aided by God, finally
attained. . . . It is amazing what this rousing of oneself

[9] Wisd. 7:8–12.

to great things can do in spiritual life." [10] Deeply rooted ideals with the firm will to realize them are a good promise of success.

c. Knowledge of God and of Self

61. Christian perfection is the soul's love of God carried to the highest degree. Love without knowledge is inconceivable. A knowledge of God and His attributes is a necessary prerequisite for Christian perfection. Such knowledge may be the result of scientific metaphysical or theological studies, or it may be the fruit of devout prayer and meditation. Relatively few persons can study theology, but everyone can pray and make short meditations on divine perfections.

The love of God goes hand in hand with self-contempt. This self-contempt is the result of self-knowledge. Without the knowledge and love of God, self-knowledge is distorted and false, characterized by pride and complacency. Self-knowledge accompanied by the knowledge of God, who is truth and goodness, produces humility and self-contempt. Man is threatened by a double peril: he may forget his own greatness and he may ignore its source. Hence Solon, one of the seven wise men of antiquity, took for his motto: Know thyself. It is a sacred duty for all mankind.

62. "Remember thy nobility and be ashamed of such a defection," says St. Bernard.[11] The loving knowledge of God and the need of self-knowledge find mystical expression, according to the interpretation of the Fathers, in

[10] *Life,* chap. 13.
[11] *De diversis ser.,* XII, 2.

the Canticle of Canticles (1:6 f.): "Show me, O thou
whom my soul loveth, where thou feedest, where thou
liest in the midday, lest I begin to wander after the flocks
of thy companions." In this verse, the bride (the soul)
asks the bridegroom (God) for divine knowledge and the
sweet repose of divine contemplation, lest she may begin
to wander "after the flocks" of created things and thus be
distracted and lose her way. The divine bridegroom tells
her that she must first learn to know herself: "If thou
know not thyself, O fairest among women, go forth, and
follow after the steps of the flocks, and feed thy kids beside the tents of the shepherds." Without self-knowledge,
the soul is not capable of divine contemplation and divine
union; all she can do is pursue created things, "follow the
steps of the flocks."

"Know thyself before anything else," says St. Nilus.
"Nothing, however, is more difficult, nothing more grievous, nothing more laborious than that. When you have
finally learnt to know yourself, then will you also be able
to know God and with your mind comprehend created
things in the proper manner." [12]

Daily examination of conscience, meditation, and spiritual retreats are the best means for the acquiring of self-
knowledge and divine knowledge as well.

d. Spiritual Readings and Instructions

63. Spiritual reading and the instructions from spiritual guides or directors are first among the exterior general
means of perfection. Spiritual reading and prayer are like
brother and sister. The reading of books in general, as we
know, greatly influences the formation of mind and char-

[12] *Epist.*, III, 314.

acter and therefore can be an important means of spiritual perfection.

64. By spiritual reading we mean, first of all, the reading of Sacred Scripture. St. Jerome is referring to this when he says, "When you read, He [God] talks to you." Next come the works of the Fathers on spiritual life and virtues, the writings of the saints and other approved spiritual writers, and the lives of the saints, whose examples are so great an inspiration.

"There is nothing that contributes so much to the life of our immortal soul as the word of God. For, as the life of the soul is increased according to the measure in which the word of God is received, grasped, and understood, so, on the other hand, a failing of that life is experienced whenever the word of God fails to be received." [13]

Spiritual instructions may be personal, like those received from one's confessor or spiritual director, or of a general nature, like those heard in a spiritual conference or sermon, in retreats, missions, and so forth. They also are the word of God. In our day the radio has become another means of hearing the word of God; and, as with books, great discretion is required in choosing only what is truly educational and inspiring.

E. SPIRITUAL DIRECTION

65. Another principal exterior means of perfection is spiritual direction. Much is said on this subject in moral theology. It should suffice here to mention that it is always useful and sometimes necessary. Too much direction is sometimes more harmful than too little. It would be an exaggeration to consider it absolutely necessary for every-

[13] St. Ambrose, *Expos. in Ps.* 118.

one. Its great usefulness, however, is based on the principle, sustained by Pope Leo XIII,[14] that it is a law of divine providence for man to be guided by other men to salvation and sanctification. The Lord sent Saul to Ananias [15] for him to learn the divine will, which God could have manifested to him directly there on the road to Damascus. But, consistent with His law—"He who heareth you heareth Me"—He sent Saul to a spiritual director for instruction and guidance. This is the common opinion of the Fathers, expressed beautifully by St. John Climacus [16] when he compares the soul to the chosen people, liberated from the slavery of Egypt under the leadership and guidance of Moses. Moses is the classical type of spiritual director.

"As a ship having a good pilot, with the help of God will reach port without any danger, so a soul, even though it has committed much evil, if it has a good shepherd, will easily reach heaven. No matter how prudent a person may be, he will easily go off the road without a guide; so also a person having all the wisdom of this world, will easily perish if in monastic life he relies only on his own judgment." [17] According to St. Bernard, whoever guides himself has a fool for a disciple.

Obviously beginners and those who have entered the mystical way need spiritual direction. Otherwise the need of a director varies greatly with individuals.

66. To be effective, spiritual direction should be accompanied by these qualities: reverence for the director, who has been chosen for his knowledge, prudence, and

---

[14] *Testem benevolentiae* (January 22, 1899).
[15] Acts 9:6 ff.
[16] *Scala paradisi.*
[17] *Ibid.*, 26.

experience; confidence in his judgment and in his intentions; docility and obedience in following his advice; and
constancy, that is, one should not change spiritual directors lightly or without grave reason.

F. RULE OF CONDUCT

67. Over and above the common rule of conduct contained in the Ten Commandments of God, the precepts
of the Church, and the special duties of our state of life,
it is helpful to have a personal and specific rule of life
for our own behavior. It should be based on the divinely
revealed rule of conduct and on our personal needs and
the special circumstances in which we live and work. It
should be shown to the spiritual director for his approval
or correction. Such a rule needs to be firm and at the same
time elastic enough to make allowance for human inconstancy and the exceptions and changes demanded either
by charity or by unforeseen circumstances.

68. This rule and the whole structure of the spiritual
formation should be based on unshakable principles,
which are the password to heaven: "My God and my all!"
(St. Francis of Assisi); *"Ad maiorem Dei gloriam"* (St.
Ignatius Loyola); *"Quid hoc ad aeternitatem?"* (St. Aloysius Gonzaga); *"Nada te turbe"* (St. Theresa). They are
fundamental truths known either by special divine illumination or perceived in the first fervor of conversion
or in meditation. They are a source of light and inspiration during life and a salutary reminder of our duty when
we tend to grow remiss.

69. The principal benefit to be derived from a rule of
conduct is a wise distribution of our time. It is amazing
how many things a person can do if he faithfully follows

a schedule. A person that never has any time has no rules or order in his life. Making a rule of life is one thing; keeping it is quite another. Punctuality, without anxiety and scrupulosity, is a prime requisite. As a certain Greek sage, Pittacos of Mitylene, advised: "Seize time by the forelock." The result is order and "order is heaven's first law" (Pope); "The friend of order has made half his way to virtue" (Lavater).

70. These six are the most common general means of perfection. Several others may be added to this list, such as the exercise of the good intention before every action, the exercise of the presence of God, the sanctification of our social relations. We regard all these as necessary parts of a truly spiritual life, but they are rather the fruit of the other general and special means of perfection. A person who is a man of prayer will of necessity remain in the presence of God, refer everything he does to a supernatural end, and sanctify his social relations.

PART II

SPECIAL ASCETICS
DEGREES IN SPIRITUAL LIFE

CHAPTER VI

THE THREE WAYS OF PERFECTION

"Show, O Lord, Thy ways to me, and teach me Thy paths." [1]

71. The ascent of the soul to God through purgation of the heart, the practice of virtue and perfect conformity with the will of God, is called the way of perfection. This section of ascetical theology is concerned with the study of this way from its very beginning to its lofty goal. The way of perfection is not always easy to follow or to travel upon. There is danger of going astray and being lost without a good knowledge of the road. The Fathers of the Church and all the saints who have traveled it have mapped it out for us, indicating all its curves, hills, detours, and the danger points. A wise person reads and studies the map before starting on a long and difficult journey. Special ascetics aims to piece together the informations left us by saints and other spiritual guides in order to form, as it were, a complete and detailed map of the road to heaven.

72. A practical method of studying a road is that of dividing it into sections. This method has been applied to the study of the way of perfection for many centuries past. It was known to pagan philosophers, such as the Neoplatonists, and to the pagan mystery cults in their initiations to perfection and deification. They spoke of

[1] Ps. 24:4.

purgation, illumination, and perfection. This idea and classification was adopted and Christianized by Pseudo-Dionysius, who attributes to both the celestial and the ecclesiastical hierarchy the threefold task of purging, illuminating, and perfecting souls.[2] In accordance with this idea, he attributes new names to deacons, priests, and bishops; deacons are called *kathartikoi* ("the purging ones"); priests are *photistikoi* ("the illuminating ones"); bishops are ἱεροτελεσταί ("sanctifying or perfecting ones"). This threefold office is exercised by the ecclesiastical hierarchy, first of all in the Christian "initiation" through baptism, confirmation, and Communion conferred upon the new member of the Church; subsequently in the spiritual formation and direction of the Christian soul in its mystical ascent to God.

73. The way of perfection had been divided into sections long before the time of Pseudo-Dionysius, and different writers gave various names to the respective parts of the way. It was about the thirteenth century, it seems, when Dionysius' nomenclature was adopted, and the way of perfection was divided into the purgative, the illuminative, and the unitive way. St. Thomas Aquinas,[3] basing his distinction on St. Gregory the Great,[4] still uses the terms "incipient," "proficient," and "perfect." St. Gregory's testimony, which St. Thomas uses, has exactly the same classification: "The beginning of virtue is one thing, its progress another, and its perfection still another." Almost identical is St. Augustine's classification. For him, Christian perfection depends entirely on charity, and

---

[2] *De eccles. hier.*, V, 3.
[3] *Summa theol.*, IIa IIae, q. 183, a. 4.
[4] *Hom.* 15 *in Ezech.*

therefore the advancement of the soul on the way of perfection is tested by its progress in love. "Initial charity is initial justice, advanced charity is advanced justice, . . . perfect charity is perfect justice." [5] More or less the same idea is expressed by St. Thomas in *III Sent.*, D. 29, a. 8, ad. 1. St. Gregory of Nyssa [6] distinguishes three degrees: fear, hope, and charity. St. John Climacus subdivides thirty degrees of his *Scala paradisi*, corresponding to the thirty rungs of the ladder by which the soul ascends to God, into three sections: the renunciation of earthly things, the extirpation of vice and acquisition of virtue, the perfect life. Cassian in his Conferences [7] has these three: the fear of slaves, the hope of mercenaries, the love of children. In his *Instituta*, however, he assigns a much greater number of degrees with no apparent reason for the distinction between one and the other. William of St. Theodoric [8] divides religious people into three classes: the animal state of the beginners, the rational state of the proficient, and the spiritual state of the perfect. St. Bonaventure [9] speaks of *via purgativa, via illuminativa,* and *via perfectiva,* not so much as degrees of perfection as being parts of meditation. Hugo de Balma, in his *Mystica theologia,* seems to be the first to have identified the terms purgative, illuminative, and unitive way with the traditional incipient, proficient, and perfect.

74. Among modern authors, O. Zimmermann [10] derives his threefold distinction from the degree of freedom of the will: the way of the commandments that oblige un-

[5] *De nat. et grat.,* 70, 84.
[6] *Hom. 1 in Cant.*
[7] *Collationes,* XI, 6–12.
[8] *Epist. ad Fratres de Monte Dei,* I, 6, n. 12.
[9] *De triplici via;* Quaracchi, VIII, 3.
[10] *Aszetik,* 20.

der grievous sin, the way of the commandments binding under venial sin, and the way of the evangelical counsels. Abbé A. Saudreau, in his *Degrees of Spiritual Life*, assigns to the purgative way, believing souls, good Christian souls; to the illuminative way, devout and fervent souls; to the unitive way, perfect souls, heroic souls, and great saints. Practically every other modern author, like A. Tanquerey (*Spiritual Life*), Meynard (*Vie intérieure*), Maval, and others, follows the division of the way of perfection into the purgative, illuminative, and unitive way, corresponding respectively to the degrees of incipient, proficient, and perfect. We shall follow this same division.

75. The reason for admitting degrees in the way of perfection, no matter what their number and name may be, is an obvious one; we cannot recommend the same specific means to all persons at all times, just as we cannot always give the same kind of food to infants, adults, and the sick or aged. This was the rule followed by St. Paul with the first Christians: "And I, brethren, could not speak to you as unto spiritual, but as unto carnal. As unto little ones in Christ. I gave you milk to drink, not meat; for you were not able as yet. But neither indeed are you now able; for you are yet carnal." [11] There is a sound analogy between the development of the supernatural, or spiritual, life and the physical life. It would be as detrimental and dangerous to apply to all and at all times the same spiritual helps as it is to give the same food to all and at all times. It was for this reason, we think, in addition to its quietist implications, that the following proposition of Michael Molinos was condemned: "The greatest

[11] I Cor. 3:1 f.

absurdity that was ever spoken of in the mystical science, is that about those three ways: the purgative, the illuminative, and the unitive way, since only one is the way, namely, the interior way." [12]

76. It is beside the point to derive the division of the three ways from the Scriptures, as has been done by Alvarez de Paz and by A. Tanquerey. The former divides the three ways according to Ps. 33:15: "Turn away from evil and do good: seek after peace and pursue it." Tanquerey [13] adds several texts from the Epistles of St. Paul, but not the text we have quoted above; and from the Synoptics he takes the words of our Lord: "If any man will come after Me, let him deny himself, and take up his cross daily, and follow Me." [14] No doubt, such texts can be beautifully adapted to the doctrine of the three ways, but they cannot be brought forward as a scriptural proof for the existence of the three ways.

77. It is well understood that when we speak of three ways, we do not mean three distinct and separate roads, starting in different directions and leading to one and the same place. We call three ways the three parts of one and the same way, the way of perfection. This is a figurative manner of saying that there are three degrees in spiritual perfection. Besides, one may reasonably consider that there are many more in spiritual perfection, but these three are the most generic and evident, and the others may be grouped under them.

The line of demarcation between one way and another is not very noticeable in the beginning, but it becomes

---

[12] Denz., 1246.
[13] *Spiritual Life*, p. 298.
[14] Luke 9:23.

more so as the soul advances. The transition is slow and not always continuous. Sometimes there are reversions to the former way. In the spiritual as in the physical life, we cannot apply mathematical measurements. The duration of the three ways depends on many circumstances and involves many elements. Chief among the latter are divine grace, the soul's generosity and fervor, its natural disposition, exterior circumstances.

78. Once the journey to perfection has been begun, there are two extremes to be avoided: remaining too little or too long on the same part of the way. There are persons who, longing for the repose of the unitive way, pass hurriedly through the purgative and illuminative, only to find that disorderly affections or bad habits have not been rooted out, and that solid virtues have not taken root in the soul at all. The discovery is disheartening and confusing. The other extreme consists in remaining much longer than necessary on the same way through indolence, sloth, or ignorance. To correct such mistakes the advice of an experienced spiritual director may be needed, for no man should be a judge in his own case.

79. The spiritual director himself may become guilty of fatal mistakes in the direction of souls on the way of perfection. The most common one consists in applying to all souls without discrimination the same standard of rules and means of perfection, for the same duration of time for all. The means of perfection recommended in ascetical and mystical theology must be applied with discretion and prudence, after making, as it were, a careful spiritual diagnosis of the subject. Only quacks pretend to cure all with the same medicine.

80. We may assign special exercises of prayer and specific acts, either of mortification or of other virtues, to each of the three ways. These forms of prayer and acts are generally but not exclusively proper to each of these ways. For example, mortification and penance are characteristic of the purgative way. From this truth we should not conclude that they no longer concern us once we are not on the purgative way. As a matter of fact, what seems to be the characteristic trait of the lowest degree of spiritual life must remain with us up to the highest degree of perfection and of the mystical graces. The other feature of the purgative way, as we shall see, is meditation or discursive prayer. This form of prayer is superseded by affective prayer and later on by contemplation, but never so as to make a return to meditation impossible or useless. That is, earlier exercises may no longer be the characteristic or specific exercises of the higher ways, but they remain as a habit, an acquired art.

CHAPTER VII

THE PURGATIVE WAY

A. Beginners in the Spiritual Life

81. "Blessed are the clean of heart: for they shall see God." [1] To "see God" is the goal of spiritual perfection, and a clean heart is the first prerequisite for the blessed vision. Spiritual perfection aims not only at the vision of God but also at union with him; and union, even more than vision, demands a perfectly pure heart and soul. The first duty, therefore, of the Christian soul striving for perfection is to purge itself of everything that offends God's sight, namely, of every sin and every sinful affection. Purging the soul of sin is as necessary as weeding the soil before planting a crop. Virtues will not grow in a sinful soul, just as no crop can thrive in a soil infested with weeds. In this section, therefore, we must point out the principal means of purging the soul from sin and disorderly affections. But first we must know what people belong to this first class.

82. In the purgative way are found only beginners in spiritual life. A beginner can be easily distinguished from other imperfect or sinful souls by his firm and sincere will to tend to perfection. Not only are obdurate sinners excluded from this class, but also all dissipated souls leading a purely sensual and natural life with no sincere desire of ever changing their conduct. Even if such persons, by

[1] Matt. 5:8.

special providence or a happy coincidence, had never committed a mortal sin, they would not even then belong to the class of beginners who have entered the purgative way, except potentially.

83. What is a beginner in the spiritual life? A beginner in spiritual life is one who lives ordinarily in the state of grace and has a sincere desire of acquiring Christian perfection and, to this end, fights against sin, struggles with more or less success against sinful affections or bad habits, and, if he should fall from time to time, rises again and is able to regain the lost ground. From this description it appears that occasional mortal sins, committed usually out of weakness and not with an evil mind, do not disprove the sincere desire of beginners to acquire perfection. Because they love God and have at least the *caritas inchoata* spoken of by St. Augustine, even their fall becomes an occasion for greater ascension in virtue, because "to them that love God, all things work together unto good," [2] even past sins. This charity of beginners is only a little fire which must be fostered and nourished lest it be extinguished. The state of beginners in the purgative way is, therefore, a state of conflict, because their principal duty is to resist their evil desires and mortify their passions. "The charity of beginners is that which, hindered by concupiscence and other passions not yet brought under control, finds neither facility nor pleasure in the exercise of virtue, and even finds itself in danger of mortal sin." [3]

84. The beginner's sincere will is not a mere wish but an efficient desire and determination to do all in his power

[2] Rom. 8:28.
[3] Suarez, *De statu religioso*, Bk. I, chap. 3.

to attain his purpose. The progress of the purgative way depends greatly on this firm determination as well as on the supernatural factor of divine grace. This determination may be called fervor or generosity, and it varies in degree so that St. Theresa placed some beginners in the first mansion of the spiritual castle and others in the second. Another reason for inequality among beginners is their past life. Some are converts who come from a life of sin and vices; some are tepid souls that never made a serious effort toward perfection, or, through negligence on the way of perfection, have fallen back to the very beginning of the road; some may be young boys or girls, still innocent and unsullied but inexperienced and susceptible to the allurements of the world.

85. Evidently these different classes of beginners cannot be subjected to the same rules. They actually belong to different degrees of the purgative way. Nor is the time required for their purgation to be measured by a common standard. Still the principal means of the purgative way are essential and ought to be applied in lesser or greater measure to all classes of beginners; such means are mental prayer, mortification, and penance. Those converted from a life of sin are ordinarily more eager for penance and mortification than those coming from a life of tepidity, but their conflicts are more numerous and more dangerous. Even those who have led an innocent life show more eagerness than veteran tepid souls.

86. Having indicated the various classes of beginners and the necessity of giving special care and attention to each class in particular, we come now to explain those fundamental means of perfection that are specific of the purgative way, namely, mental prayer and mortification.

The mental prayer for the purgative way is the first of
its kind and is called meditation. Mortification includes
also penance and the struggle against temptations and the
capital sins.

B. MEDITATION

87. Mental prayer is commonly defined as "the raising
of the mind and heart to God." This definition was known
long before St. John Damascene, to whom it is often attributed.[4] St. Nilus (d. 430) had already defined prayer
as an "ascent of the mind to God." [5] This definition fits all
forms of mental prayer because all are an ascent or the
raising of the mind and heart to God. It is the degree of
difficulty encountered by the mind in this ascent which
indicates the various forms of mental prayer and almost
without exception the degree of spiritual perfection of the
soul itself as well.

88. In chapter five we touched upon the necessity of
prayer in general as a means of salvation and sanctification. What has been said there applies to meditation and
mental prayer also. Mental prayer is a necessary means
of Christian perfection. It is the very soul of spiritual life,
the motive-power of all spiritual progress. No more effi-
cacious means for perseverance in divine grace and in the
abhorrence of mortal sin can be suggested than daily
meditation. "In mental prayer it is God who speaks to us:
'I will lead her into the wilderness, and I will speak to her
heart.' [6] Now, God speaks better than any preacher. It is
by the practice of mental prayer that all the saints have

[4] *De fide orthodoxa,* III, 24.
[5] *De oratione,* chap. 35.
[6] Osee 2:14.

been sanctified. Experience proves that those who are faithful to prayer are preserved from mortal sin; or, if they should happen to fall, they promptly rise again. Mental prayer and mortal sin are incompatible. Many Christians fast and recite the rosary or the Office of Our Lady, and yet continue to live in sin; whereas he who remains faithful to mental prayer will not only abandon sin, but he will detach his heart from all creatures in order that he may love God alone. Prayer is the furnace in which souls are fired with the divine love." [7] No one who perseveres in mental prayer will remain in mortal sin. If, therefore, so much sin is rampant and the world at large is in a state of spiritual desolation, it is because, as Jeremias complained, nobody meditates in his heart.

c. TYPES OF MENTAL PRAYER

89. According to the common teaching of spiritual writers and theologians, each of the three ways or degrees of perfection corresponds to a special form or degree of mental prayer: the purgative way corresponds to meditation; the illuminative way to affective prayer; the unitive way to contemplation. Contemplation is of two kinds: the ordinary which is called acquired contemplation, and the extraordinary, called infused contemplation. These two forms of contemplation correspond to two different unitive ways: the ascetical and the mystical. "Meditation or discursive prayer is proper to beginners who are in the purgative way; affective prayer to those who are advancing and are in the illuminative way; contemplation and the prayer of union to the perfect who are in the unitive

[7] St. Alphonsus, *Praxis conf.*, 217.

way." [8] The same is the division given by J. J. Surin in his *Catéchisme Spirituel:* "For whom is discursive prayer? For beginners. For whom affective prayer? For those who advance. For whom is contemplation? For the perfect." [9] In the following chapter he speaks of the two kinds of contemplation mentioned above. All these various forms of mental prayer are an elevation of heart and mind to God, but each is more simple and perfect than the preceding one. The first is called discursive prayer because of the predominant mental process, in search of truth and light; the second is called affective prayer because the will predominates over the mind, the affections over the considerations; the third is called contemplation because it is a simple, unclouded, loving regard of divine things.

D. HISTORY OF MENTAL PRAYER

90. Mental prayer as an elevation of heart and mind to God, without a special form or method, is as old as mankind itself and it was surely practiced by our first parents both in Paradise and after their fall. As far as it can be ascertained, it remained so until the fifteenth, or even the sixteenth century of our Christian era, when fixed rules and method were introduced, especially by St. Ignatius. Such rules concern first of all discursive prayer or meditation and affective prayer and, to a lesser extent, the acquired contemplation. Infused contemplation, however, is beyond all human rules and methods, and it remains so today as it was in the Garden of Eden. With a fixed method for mental prayer, it was found necessary to de-

[8] L. Lallemant, 7^e *principe,* chap. 1.
[9] Part I, chap. 1.

termine in advance its subject and duration. The rules for religious before this period contained no definite instructions with regard to mental prayer, except the injunction to be recollected and to occupy their thoughts with God and His divine law during their spare time. The word "meditation" was not restricted to mental prayer in ancient times; it often meant simply pious reading or study, as in the Rule of St. Benedict (chapter 8, *De officiis divinis in noctibus*). In winter his religious must rise early, "about the eighth hour of the night," in order to sing Matins. According to the Latin text of the Rule, the time that remains after Matins should be employed in meditation.[10] Since the sixteenth century, the older Orders have introduced at least a half-hour of mental prayer a day; and all religious societies and congregations founded since that time prescribe daily meditations, an obligation made mandatory by the Code of Canon Law (can. 595, 2). The same code directs bishops to see that secular priests also devote a certain time each day to the pious exercise of mental prayer (can. 125, 2).

E. DEFINITION OF MENTAL PRAYER

91. Meditation is a pious and profound consideration of divine truths with the purpose of amending our life and conforming it to the will of God. From this definition it appears that meditation is the combined work of mind and will and, instrumentally, of the memory, imagination, emotions, and so on. The entire soul is occupied in it in a logical and orderly way. From this alone it is evident

---

[10] *Quod vero restat post vigilias a fratribus qui Psalterii vel lectionum aliquid indigent meditationi inserviatur.* Here *meditatio* probably means learning the psalms (i.e., by heart) and learning to read the lessons.

what a potent factor meditation is in the purgation and sanctification of the soul. The searching mind throws light in dark recesses of the heart; things heretofore unnoticed appear in all their ugliness or beauty; the will is stirred; the heart is touched; resolutions are taken, while humble prayer is addressed to God, asking for pardon and divine assistance.

Meditation is first of all a consideration by the mind, a consideration that is careful and profound. Not every careful and profound consideration of divine truths is a meditation; it may be theological study if dissociated from the practical aim of moving the will to take firm resolutions and amending its ways or of practicing some special virtue. Therefore the consideration of the intellect must be not only profound but pious, that is, it must tend to the purgation and sanctification of the soul.

The purpose of meditation is to turn the soul away from sin and incline it to virtue. The important step must be taken by the will, which is a blind faculty that must be guided by the light of the mind in order to see its object. Whatever is good is the object of the will. Sin and disorder enter whenever the will, through misinformation of the senses, loves what is good only in appearance but not in reality. Sin is actually a deception. When the real truth is made manifest with the help of divine grace, the attitude of the will eventually changes. Meditation is necessary for conversion from sin and also for perseverance in the good resolutions taken. Amendment of the will is the general fruit to be derived from every meditation, but a meditation would not be considered practical if it did not in addition produce a more specific effect, like the avoidance of a definite fault or the acquisition of a partic-

ular virtue. This is called the particular fruit of meditation. For example, the general fruit of a meditation on
death might be a general detachment of the heart from
everything that is transitory and that ends with death;
the particular fruit would be a detachment from a person
or a thing that has been occasion of sin in the past.

f. Method of Meditation

92. St. Ignatius Loyola in his *Spiritual Exercises* offers
several methods of mental prayer. The one best adapted
for the beginners of the purgative way is the method
called the exercise of the three faculties, namely, the intellect, the will, and the memory, the three principal faculties of the soul. It is a powerful array of psychological
forces which, assisted by divine grace, is able to break
even inveterate sinners that have at least a vestige of good
will left in them. In the exercise of the three faculties some
rules must be observed before meditation, some during
meditation, and some after meditation.

93. Before meditation. 1. Remote preparation. The
subject of meditation should be chosen and be divided
into two or three points. Beginners should make use of
meditation books in which such division is already made.
If meditation is made in the morning, the remote preparation should be made the evening before, by determining
the special fruit to be derived and by impressing the subject upon the mind.

2. Proximate preparation. Immediately before meditation itself, a preparatory prayer is humbly recited, in
which we beg God for His grace to direct and assist all
the faculties and operations of our soul to His glory and
our sanctification.

3. Preludes. A prelude in music is a short introduction which aims to prepare the ear to the tempo and tonality of the composition that follows. In meditation our memory and imagination play the same role in preparing the mind and the heart for the meditation that follows. The preludes are ordinarily two. The first is called the *compositio loci*. In it the imagination seizes the object of meditation by placing it in a certain spot which the mind represents to itself or which is indicated by the historical fact or mystery of the meditation. In meditating on the life of our Savior the place is always indicated by the text or context of the meditation. On purely intellectual truths the mind must supply the equivalent of place. The purpose of this prelude is to give the soul the impression of being present at the mystery where and when it occurred. In the second prelude we determine and propose once more the special fruit to be derived from meditation and pray that God may grant it to us.

All these preparatory acts should take a very short time. If for lack of imagination a person does not succeed in the first prelude, he should waste no time in useless efforts but proceed to the second.

94. During meditation. It is here that the three faculties of the soul are exercised. The memory, with the assistance of the imagination, places before the mind the mystery or the truth which is the subject of the meditation. If we make use of a book, the work of the memory is greatly facilitated. The mind or intellect considers the proposed subject carefully from various angles in order to make practical reflections. The different circumstances to be considered are comprised in that famous Latin verse:

Quis, quid, ubi, per quos, quoties, cur, quomodo, quando (who, what, where, by whom, how often, why, how, when).

When sufficient consideration has been given one point, the intellect must proceed to draw practical conclusions and apply them to the present needs of the soul. This practical application implies a sort of examination of conscience: we examine our conduct and compare it with the pattern of virtue and perfection just considered and notice how far we still are from it. Having thus seen our defects, we must humbly confess them before God and make a firm resolution to correct them. This resolution is the work of the will; and it must be real and specific. It would not be very practical if one should resolve, in a general way, not to sin any more, to become better, or the like. The resolution must be well defined as to nature, time, place, and other circumstances. In making it, the mind should consider the motives and the means for keeping it, and the whole soul should pray for the necessary grace. Prayer and affections should follow and accompany the applications and resolutions. These prayers and affections may be formulated either with a known vocal prayer, like the *Miserere, De profundis,* Our Father, and so on, or they may be improvised, expressing in our own words, our sorrow, shame, gratitude, love, faith, and the like.

95. After meditation. The meditation is concluded with colloquies with the three Persons of the Blessed Trinity, with the Blessed Virgin, and patron saints, followed by a short review of the meditation and especially of the resolutions that have been taken. The review has the purpose of examining how the meditation has succeeded. If it has not, through negligence or for some similar reason, we should repent and make firm resolutions for the future. In this way we learn the art of meditation.

96. From this summary view of meditation, it appears that the entire soul is engaged in it. The various faculties should be occupied in it no more and no longer than necessary, otherwise distractions may follow; and if meditation is not well proportioned, it loses its efficacy. Memory and intellect should dwell on the subject only as long as is necessary to move the will and the heart to action. After all, the reason why we meditate is to correct our will, to detach it from evil and incline it to good. After the first point has been exhausted, we should pass to the next. If we find in a single point enough spiritual food to last for the prescribed time of meditation, there is no reason for abandoning it. The longer we can linger, with spiritual profit, on one point or one thought, the more perfect is our mental prayer.

97. Meditation, as explained above, is the perfect form of methodical prayer, a perfection reached in the *Spiritual Exercises* of St. Ignatius of Loyola in the first quarter of the sixteenth century. But attempts to bring some method and system to mental prayer were made more than one century before St. Ignatius. In fact, St. Bonaventure himself (in the *De triplici via*) recommends meditation and gives some general rules for making it. The Franciscan School followed St. Bonaventure in this matter and developed his method to some extent. When, at the end of the Middle Ages, the worldliness and laxity of the pagan Renaissance superseded the simple, living faith of the preceding era and invaded even the clergy and the religious orders, methodical prayer was resorted to as a means of reform. It was thought powerful enough to restore in them the life of the spirit. To this end, during the fifteenth century several collections of pious exercises for every day of the week were published under the name of *Exercitatoria.* The most celebrated and practical *Exercitatorium* was that of the Benedictine Garcia Ximenes de Cisneros, abbot of Montserrat in Spain, 1475–1510. He succeeded in reforming his monks by making them follow his exercises, published under the title of *Ejercitatorio de la vida espiritual.* In 1522 Ignatius Loyola came to visit the shrine of Our Lady of Montserrat after his conversion and to make a general confession there. His spiritual director, a Benedictine of the Abbey, probably gave the future author of the *Spiritual Exercises* a copy of the *Ejercitatorio* of Abbot Cisneros. In spite of the originality of method displayed by Ignatius with regard to spiritual exercises and meditation, it cannot be denied that his inspiration derived from the method followed at the Abbey of Montserrat.[11]

98. St. Theresa's description (in her *Life,* the *Way of Perfection,* and the *Interior Castle,* or *Mansions*) of the different degrees of prayer as so many stages which she herself passed through completes and enlarges the method of mental prayer of the ascetical and mystical ways and makes it more attractive and popular even among lay people. St. Theresa's contribution to the art of mental prayer is unique and supreme especially in the various forms and degrees of contemplation.

99. After that classical epoch of mental prayer there was a period of imitation and decadence, which naturally

[11] Pourrat, *Christian Spirituality,* III, 1 f.

follows when people try to outdo what is universally considered perfect. The method introduced by the French School, the Berullian method and its various imitations, may appeal to some people, but not to the majority and certainly not to beginners. The Sulpician method of meditation [12] is based on the Berullian principle of devotion and adherence to the Word incarnate, a principle expressed sometimes with the word "Christocentric." This method of mental prayer, despite the additions of Father Tronson, is better adapted for those who are in the illuminative way than for beginners of the purgative way. After the ordinary preparation, the Suplician method divides the body of meditation into three points. The first point is adoration, or "Jesus before our eyes," the second is communion, or "Jesus in our heart," the third is cooperation, or "Jesus in our hands." Then comes the conclusion, which resembles the colloquies of the Ignatian method. As it appears, this method of prayer presupposes a kind of intimacy with our Savior, which is not common in the beginning of the purgative way, when the mind predominates over the heart, truth over love. The Ignatian method is eminently psychological; it forces man to enter into himself and behold his misery and desolation and cry to heaven for help and assistance; the Sulpician method is more devotional and objective.

100. The time to be employed in meditation depends on many circumstances. As a rule, a good meditation requires at least half an hour. Religious are governed by their rule in this respect. The secular clergy are required to attend to mental prayer daily *per aliquod tempus* (can. 125, 2). The meditation of a point would require at least

[12] Tanquerey, *The Spiritual Life*, pp. 335 ff.

one quarter of an hour, and no meditation can be performed in less time than this.

101. Meditation is often the source of great spiritual joy and consolation, which foster the detachment of the soul from sinful affections, but sometimes aridity and distraction are experienced instead. In such case meditation becomes a burden and one may be tempted to shorten it or to drop it completely. This would be a great mistake and a misfortune. Constancy and perseverance, in spite of all obstacles, will be often of greater spiritual advantage than all the sweetness of the spiritual consolations. But, whether in consolation or in aridity, what David experienced always remains true of our meditation: "My heart grew hot within me: and in my meditation a fire shall flame out. I spoke with my tongue: O Lord, make me know my end, and what is the number of my days: that I may know what is wanting to me." [13]

That meditation may become a practical means of perfection, we should follow the advice of St. Theresa of Avila: "Keep present before you all day what you meditate upon in the morning, and use much diligence in this point, for it will be of great benefit to you. Observe carefully the thoughts with which our Lord may inspire you, and execute the desires which He shall give you in prayer." [14]

[13] Ps. 38:4 f.
[14] *Advices of the Holy Mother Teresa of Jesus for Her Nuns*, pp. 31 f.

*Read +
learn main
points.*

CHAPTER VIII

MORTIFICATION AND PENANCES

A. DEFINITION

102. Mortification is both spiritual and physical self-discipline, denoting the inner curbing of self-love and self-inflicted bodily austerities. When these austerities are practiced to expiate past sins, they are more commonly called penances.

Next to mental prayer, mortification is the most necessary means of purification. It cuts the soul free from sin. This violent and often painful operation is made possible and easy through meditation and the grace of God. Mortification breaks the bad habits and opens the door to good ones. Rather than a specific virtue, it is the sum total of all those efforts that are needed to subdue and correct the inordinate inclinations of our fallen nature. The whole ascetic teaching of Christ is summed up in a forceful exhortation to self-denial and mortification: "If any man will come after Me, let him deny himself and take up his cross daily and follow Me."[1] Sacred Scripture designates mortification by many names, each of which reveals a new aspect of the thing itself. It is called self-denial: as in the text just quoted. In the same text, the "cross" is another name for mortification. It is hate of self: "He that hateth his life in this world, keepeth

[1] Luke 9:23.

91

it unto life eternal." [2] St. Paul calls it a stripping of self: "stripping yourselves of the old man"; [3] a crucifixion: "they that are Christ's have crucified their flesh, with the vices and concupiscences"; [4] and lastly, mortification: "mortify your members which are upon the earth." [5] The Latin etymology of the word is *mortuum facere,* to make one as though dead. This death or killing, brought about by mortification, is a mystical death, a death to sin. Without this death there can be no life in Christ, much less perfection of that life: "Dead to sin, but alive unto God, in Christ Jesus our Lord." [6]

103. Mortification is, therefore, the abc of spiritual life. No one can be called spiritual who does not practice mortification and mental prayer. These are the two feet on which one walks on the way of perfection. Mortification depends on prayer, and prayer on mortification; one helps the other and is kept going by the other. They are like two wings: one would be helpless without the other. Theirs is a team-work. Nothing is more emphasized in the Gospel and in the doctrine of the apostles than the need of prayer and mortification. The various names for the latter in Sacred Scripture not only explain its nature, but also manifest its necessity, coming from the ever-present danger of sin, the major cause of which is within ourselves in our fallen nature. Since the first sin of Adam, when sin entered into this world, man has been at war with it as his deadly enemy; it is spiritual death. The soldier on the battlefield must be well armed and he must

[2] John 12:25.
[3] Col. 3:9.
[4] Gal. 5:24.
[5] Col. 3:5.
[6] Rom. 6:11.

watch, pray. Mortification together with prayer offers the necessary armor for defense and attack. The two camps in this war are the flesh and the spirit, or the body and the soul. "The wisdom of the flesh is death; but the wisdom of the spirit is life and peace. . . . For if you live according to the flesh, you shall die: but if by the Spirit you mortify the deeds of the flesh, you shall live." [7] The purpose of mortification, however, is not the death and ruin of the body but its subjection: "I chastise my body, and bring it into subjection: lest perhaps, when I have preached to others, I myself should become a castaway." [8] As already stated elsewhere, our nature is substantially good, but a great disorder and weakness followed the fall of man. It is against this disorder and weakness that mortification must be directed.

B. OBJECT

104. The object of mortification is all that is rebellious and disorderly in our nature: the passions and appetites when they are inspired by self-love. Love of oneself, if not restrained by mortification, will lead to contempt of all human and divine laws and finally of God Himself. In the two opposed camps, or cities, as St. Augustine calls them, we have two kinds of love fighting each other: the love of self and the love of God, as St. Augustine says: "Two loves have given origin to these two cities: self-love in contempt of God unto the earthly, love of God in contempt of one's self to the heavenly." [9] The author of the *Imitation of Christ* considers self-love man's worst

[7] Rom. 8:6, 13.
[8] I Cor. 9:27.
[9] *De Civit. Dei*, XIV, 28.

enemy in this world: "Know that the love of thyself hurts thee more than anything in the world." [10] Self-love never completely dies, hence the necessity of unremitting mortification for all. It manifests itself not only in what is sinful and vicious but also in what appears to be virtuous and perfect; in all things it strives to take the place of God. Since the duty of mortification is to substitute God and the salvation of our soul for self-love, we call it abnegation and self-denial. Self-love is opposed to charity, the queen of all virtues, and therefore to Christian perfection. It is contrary to the love of God and of our neighbor and even to the supernatural and well-ordered love of self, for it is the chief reason why souls are lost: "He that loveth his life shall lose it, and he that hateth his life in this world, keepeth it unto life eternal." [11] Mortification is not hatred of self but the only true love of self in this life.

c. Errors Regarding Mortification

105. Quietists considered mortification superfluous and useless. This idea is contained in the following propositions of Molinos, condemned by Innocent XI: "The voluntary cross of mortifications is a heavy and fruitless burden; therefore it must be given up. The holiest works and penances performed by the saints are not sufficient to remove even a single attachment from the soul." [12] A recent Catholic writer has said that sin is only a secondary reason for mortification and that mortification would be necessary even if there were no actual sin, for we must

---

[10] *Imitation,* III, 27.
[11] John 12:25.
[12] Denz., 1258, 1259.

die, not merely to sin, but to the natural. Here the question does not concern the necessity of mortification, on which we all agree, but its motive. We do not practice mortification for mortification's sake. It is a bitter and unpleasant thing. We do not take a distasteful medicine for its own sake, but to regain health. Mortification has the same function: we practice it because of sin, which is a deadly disease of the soul. If there were no sin or danger of sin, there would be no reason for mortification. To say that one must die "not merely to sin but to the natural" seems to imply that, apart from sin, nature is evil. We have already mentioned the danger of such an extreme opinion. The purpose of mortification is to subject nature and make it serve justice; and, with the grace of God, our fallen human nature is still able to do that.

d. Interior and Exterior Mortification

106. Mortification has to be directed against all manifestations and expressions of self-love. Some such expressions are interior, in the judgment, will, feelings, memory, and imagination. If not restrained by mortification, such expressions of self-love are either sins or the cause of sin. This kind of mortification is called interior, because of its object. It might be called the mortification of the soul, in contrast to exterior mortification, which is the mortification of the body in all its senses. To this must be added the mortification of the tongue. Interior mortification comes first. Without it the exterior would be useless and false. The interior is more necessary and of a higher nature than the exterior, and, being unseen, passes unnoticed and so cannot become a source of pride and vanity. Exterior or bodily mortification is often necessary for the avoidance of sin and always useful. It assists the soul in prayer and cooperates with interior mortification. The mortification of the tongue, of the eyes, and of hearing are necessary for recollection and peace of mind. In the mortification of the senses we need to proceed systematically and untiringly and to avoid extremes. The golden rule in mortification is moderation and perseverance. Thus mortification will not injure our health; on the contrary, it will protect it. The continual exercise of mortification will strengthen our will against temptations and make it always ready for the practice of Christian virtues. We proceed systematically in mortifying ourselves when we attack first the vice or defect that is the usual cause of our falls; when one defect has been conquered, mortification is directed against another.

107. Both interior and exterior mortification may be positive and negative; that is, self-discipline or the patient endurance of all the unpleasant things that happen without our looking for them. The acceptance of difficulties connected with our work or vocation, with the fulfillment of our duties toward God and man, is in the category of passive mortification. This should come first, for it would profit us nothing to mortify our senses and at the same time be very impatient, remiss, and full of complaint in our work. The well-known spiritual advice, *abstine et sustine,* expresses these two forms of mortification.

108. Generous souls are not satisfied with what is indispensable in interior and exterior mortification; they practice great austerities, like fasting, shortening their sleep, resting on the hard ground or a hard bed, wearing penitential garbs and instruments, scourging themselves,

and so on. For this kind of mortification a person should always obtain the sanction of his spiritual director and be guided by obedience, because by indiscreet zeal he may ruin his health and frustrate the purpose of mortification. If such austerities are practiced for expiation, to atone for past sins, they are usually called penances. Not only sinners but also innocent souls have often practiced such austerities after the example of our Savior. Without being evil in itself, the body often proves to be the enemy of our soul and the main source of temptations and disturbing emotions. Therefore the saints have given their bodies only what was necessary to keep them alive: "By going away to the Lord, for the love he [the gnostic, i.e., the perfect Christian] bears Him, though his tabernacle can be seen on earth, he does not betake himself out of life. For that is not permitted to him. But he has withdrawn his soul from the passions. For that is granted to him. And, on the other hand, he lives, having put to death his lusts, and no longer makes use of the body, but allows it the use of necessaries, that he may not give cause for dissolution." [13]

109. This "going away to the Lord, for the love he bears Him" is self-denial and mortification, based on the love of God as opposed to self-love. St. Augustine's words on this subject are beautiful: "Man's first ruin was the love of himself. For if he had not loved himself, if he had preferred God to himself, he would have been willing to be ever subject to God, and would not have been turned to the neglect of His will, and the doing of his own will. For this is to love one's self, to wish to do one's

[13] Clement of Alexandria, *Strom.*, VI, 9.

own will. Prefer to this God's will; learn to love thyself by not loving thyself." [14]

110. Self-denial or mortification in all its forms and aspects is the chief contributing factor in the active purgation of the soul. No union with God is possible without purgation of the senses and of the spirit. When God guides a soul to mystical union, He makes that soul go through a series of passive purgations, which were called the dark night of the senses and the dark night of the spirit by St. John of the Cross. Ordinary union with God, outside the mystical union, requires a similar purgation of the senses and the spirit. This purgation may be active and passive. Active purgation consists chiefly in mortifications and penances as described above. Passive purgation consists in the humble and patient acceptance of all kinds of trials, like aridities, temptations, contradictions, misunderstandings, false accusations, persecutions, and long and painful maladies. This latter form of purgation extends beyond the purgative way and disposes the soul for the perfect union with God.

111. "The reason why it is necessary for the soul, in order to attain to divine union with God, to pass through this dark night of mortification of the appetites and denial of pleasures in all things, is that all the affections it has for creatures are nothing but darkness in the eyes of God, and, when the soul is clothed in these affections, it has no capacity for being illumined and possessed by the pure and simple light of God if it cast them not first from it, for the light cannot agree with darkness; since, as St. John says, 'the darkness did not comprehend it.' That is, the darkness could not receive the light. . . . We must

[14] Sermon 46, 2.

know that the affection and attachment which the soul has for creatures make the soul like these creatures; and the greater is the affection, the closer is the equality and resemblance between them; for love creates a resemblance between the lover and the beloved. For this reason, David, speaking of those who set their affections upon idols, said: 'Let them that make them become like unto them; and all such as trust in them.' [15] This means: Let them that set their heart upon them be like to them. And thus he that loves a creature becomes as low as that creature, and, in some ways, lower, for love not only makes the lover equal to the object of his love, but even subjects him to it. Wherefore in the same way it happens that the soul that loves anything else becomes incapable of pure union with God and transformation in Him. For the lowliness of the creature is much less capable of union with the high estate of the Creator than is darkness with light." [16]

112. It seems fitting to conclude this chapter on mortification with some of the spiritual counsels of St. John of the Cross.

To arrive at having pleasure in everything, desire to have pleasure in nothing.

To arrive at possessing everything, desire to possess nothing.

To arrive at being everything, desire to be nothing.

To arrive at that wherein thou hast no pleasure, thou must go by a way wherein thou hast no pleasure.

To arrive at that which thou possessest not, thou must go by a way of possessing nothing.

To arrive at that which thou art not, thou must go through that which thou art not.[17]

[15] Ps. 113:8.
[16] St. John of the Cross, *The Ascent of Mount Carmel*, I, 4.
[17] *Ibid.*, chap. 13.

CHAPTER IX

TEMPTATIONS

THE PARTICULAR EXAMINATION

A. DEFINITION OF TEMPTATION

113. Temptation is a more or less violent enticement to evil. "The life of man upon earth is a warfare." [1] According to the Septuagint version, it is a temptation.[2] But if all life is warfare, temptation is a particular battle, a specific attack of the enemy. Generally speaking, to tempt a person is to test him, to find out whether he knows, whether he is able or willing. From our point of view, temptation consists usually in getting man's attention and then his consent. It is one of the great obstacles on the way of perfection. It is a crisis in spiritual life and sometimes the beginning of spiritual ruin.

114. Of all the Fathers none has better expounded or more deeply analyzed the nature of temptaton than St. Augustine. The Fathers of the desert were inclined to see the devil in all their temptations. St. Augustine, while not denying the devil's agency, reduces it to its proper proportions. The main source of man's temptations lies in man himself, in his concupiscence. This is the teaching of the Apostle St. James: "Every man is tempted by his own concupiscence, being drawn away and allured. Then

[1] Job 7:1.
[2] The word in the Greek text is πειρατήριον.

when concupiscence hath conceived, it bringeth forth
sin. But sin, when it is completed, begetteth death." [3] According to St. John's First Epistle,[4] this concupiscence
arises from the lust of the flesh, from pride, and from
curiosity. St. Augustine translates St. John's *concupiscen-
tia oculorum* as curiosity: "These three kinds of vice,
namely, the pleasure of the flesh, and pride, and curiosity,
include all sins." [5] God Himself does not tempt man in
the proper sense of the word, because temptation is an
inducement to sin; but God permits man to be tempted
on occasion, making provision that he may resist and
win and so acquire a new crown of victory. When God
is said to tempt man, as He did with Abraham, He does
so to try and strengthen his faith.

115. The pattern of all temptations is found in the first,
which led to original sin: first, the serpent's suggestions
and insinuations proposing disobedience to God's com-
mands by eating the forbidden fruit; then Eve's curiosity
and pleasure regarding the forbidden fruit; finally the
transgression. Similarly, in every enticement to evil, we
have first the mere suggestion or thought of it in the soul.
Then the imagination proceeds to represent more or less
vividly the suggested action. The image of the action
sometimes impresses itself so deeply on the mind as to become almost an obsession. As it were instinctively, concupiscence is excited, adding delight and pleasure to the
thought of the evil suggested and influencing the will to
yield. Up to this point we have temptation only, and not
sin. The instinctive pleasures excited in the lower nature

[3] Jas. 1:14 f.
[4] I John 2:15 f.
[5] *Enarr. in Psal.*, 8, no. 13.

by concupiscence at the suggestion and representation of the evil action are not sin. And this is extremely important to remember. If the will yields and consents to temptation by approving what is suggested, then sin is committed. If the will refuses, a victory is won in spite of the feeling of rebellion and pleasure experienced in the lower appetites at the suggestion of sin. This, in a few words, is the psychological analysis of temptation made by St. Augustine.[6]

116. Formal sin is in the will and in the will alone, not in the flesh or in the imagination. It is through his will that man turns away from God and sins. While he resists the evil suggestions, he may feel pleasure. Feelings are not dependent upon the will, and consequently the person is not responsible for them. During the sack of Rome in 410, many Christian women and virgins were violated by the invaders. To reassure and comfort the victims of these outrages, St. Augustine, who about this time was writing his *City of God,* stresses the difference between consent and feelings of pleasure, and the fact that both virtue and sin are in the soul, not in the body:

Let this, then, first be laid down and affirmed: virtue is enthroned in the soul, whence it rules the members of the body, which remains holy so long as the will which regulates its motions is holy. As long as the will remains firm and unshaken, any violence that another person does upon the body does not render us culpable, so long as we cannot escape it without committing sin. But as it is possible by certain acts not only to inflict pain upon the body of another, but also to gratify lust, whenever anything of this kind takes place, even though it does not destroy the modesty which a firm virtue never loses, it yet creates a feeling of shame, lest people should think that an act which could not perhaps be

[6] *Ibid.,* 90, no. 7; 143, no. 6.

done without giving some pleasure to the flesh was also committed
with some assent of the will. . . . Modesty is a virtue of the soul
and has for its companion virtue the fortitude that resolves to endure all evils rather than to consent to evil. But since no one is
always the master of his own body, however courageous and modest he may be, but can only control the consent and refusal of his
will, what man in his senses can suppose that his modesty is lost if
perchance his body be forcibly seized for the exercise and satisfaction of another's lust? [7]

117. The present life is the time of trial; consequently
temptations are unavoidable. Man must be tried and
tested in this life; he must fight before he can receive
the crown of victory, but nobody can be tried without
temptation. When we are admonished to ask in the Lord's
Prayer, "Lead us not into temptation," we are not asking
that we be exempt from temptations, but that we may
not fall when we are tempted.

God does not Himself lead, but suffers that man be led into temptation whom he has deprived of his assistance, in accordance with a
most hidden arrangement, and with his deserts. Often also, for
manifest reasons, he judges him worthy of being so deprived, and
allowed to be led into temptation. But it is one thing to be led into
temptation, another to be tempted. For without temptation no one
can be proved, whether to himself, as it is written, "He that hath
not been tempted, what doth he know?" [8] or to another, as the
Apostle says, "And your temptation in my flesh you despised not," [9]
for from this circumstance he learnt that they were steadfast, because they were not turned aside from charity by those tribula-
tions which had happened to the Apostle according to the flesh. For
even before all temptations we are known to God, who knows all
things before they happen. . . . Here, therefore, the prayer is not
that we should not be tempted, but that we should not be led into

[7] *De Civit. Dei*, I, 16.
[8] Ecclus., 34:9.
[9] Gal. 4:13.

temptation: as if, were it necessary that anyone should be examined by fire, he should pray, not that he should not be touched by fire, but that he should not be consumed.[10]

118. St. Augustine explains the same doctrine more in detail in his seventh sermon:

"Lead us not into temptation, but deliver us from evil." Will this again be necessary in the life to come? "Lead us not into temptation," will not be said except where there can be temptation. We read in the book of holy Job, "Is not the life of man upon earth a temptation," What, then, do we pray for? Hear what. The Apostle James says: "Let no man say when he is tempted, I am tempted of God." [11] He spoke of those evil temptations whereby men are deceived and brought under the yoke of the devil. This is the kind of temptation he spoke of. For there is another sort of temptation which is called a proving; of this kind of temptation it is written: "The Lord your God trieth you [tempteth you] that it may appear whether you love Him." [12] What is meant by "to know," "to make you know"? For He knows already. What that kind of temptation, where we are deceived and seduced? God does not tempt anyone. But undoubtedly in His deep and hidden judgment He abandons some. And after He has abandoned them, the tempter finds his opportunity. For he finds in him no resistance against his power, but forthwith presents himself to him as his possessor, if God abandon him. Therefore that He may not abandon us do we say: "Lead us not into temptation."

b. Usefulness of Temptations

119. By resisting temptations a Christian turns them to his own spiritual advantage and profit. They purify the soul. The passive purgation consists of all sorts of trials and temptations. Since our Lord Himself was tempted, it cannot be considered a disgrace to be tempted. The

[10] St. Augustine, *De serm. Dom. in monte,* II, 30, 32.
[11] Jas. 1:13.
[12] Deut. 13:3.

greatest saints had the greatest temptations. Only strong and valiant soldiers are placed where the assault of the enemy is most deadly. Habitual sinners do not grasp the significance of temptation because they gladly accept any invitation to evil. Temptation is not a sign of perversion but of virtue. After the temptation has met repeated refusals, it begins to lose its power to attract or seduce, and thus the soul is purified.

Temptation teaches us. It reveals to us our true condition, our fallen nature; it shows what our inclinations are, what we are able to do, how exposed we are to the enemies of virtue and holiness. In the fervor of the spirit and the mystical elevation of the soul, a person may forget what he really is; temptation serves as a reminder. This was the case with St. Paul the Apostle. After his heavenly revelations and assumption to the third heaven, he suffered temptations of the flesh: "Lest the greatness of the revelations should exalt me." [13] Temptation advances us in virtue and perfection. Many a virtue must be practiced in order to overcome temptation. In addition to the virtue attacked by the temptation, we practice the theological virtues of faith, hope, and charity, and also patience, often to a high degree. Humility and the fear of God are strenghtened by the presence of temptation, and sanctifying grace is increased in the soul that has remained faithful throughout the trial. Lastly, temptation induces man to pray and to watch over his senses. Man would easily forget prayer if there were no temptation. [14]

120. St. Thomas, explaining the words of St. Matthew, "Then Jesus was led by the spirit into the desert, to be

[13] II Cor. 12:7.
[14] St. Augustine, *Epist.*, 130, 5.

tempted by the devil," [15] adds two other reasons why a
Christian is tempted after he has received spiritual grace.
One is the greater confusion of the devil in discovering
the power of Christ, whom he cannot conquer; an example
of this is Job: "Hast thou considered My servant Job?" [16]
Another reason is that man may recognize his own dignity,
because it is an honor for him to be attacked by the enemy
of God, the devil.

Although the spiritual advantages that may be derived
from temptation are many, it is not advisable to seek it,
because its usefulness is not absolute but, of course, merely
contingent. In the absolute sense of the term, temptation
is neither good nor useful. Of itself it tends to evil. Through
the grace of God and man's cooperation, it becomes an
opportunity to practice virtue and acquire spiritual profit.
For many, however, it is the occasion of spiritual ruin and
death.

c. Kinds of Temptation

121. In passive purgation, the common temptation is
not a positive enticement to evil, but rather the omission
of good works and pious practices. This is especially the
case in time of spiritual desolation and aridity. The devil
cannot force our will in spite of itself. He proceeds as he
did with Eve by way of seduction, using whatever unruly
appetite we have within us and taking advantage of the
actual inclinations of the soul. The devil's suggestions
spring from two main sources or human passions, namely,
love of pleasure and fear of pain. The diabolic influence,
in this respect, is not always direct. The bad example of

[15] Matt. 4:1.
[16] Job 1:8.

evil men and the seduction of the world are employed by
the devil to weaken the mind. He sometimes resorts to
obsession, a means often employed by him against the
Fathers of the desert, as we read in the lives of Anthony,
Hilarion, and Pachomius.[17] According to Cassian: "All
men are tempted for one of these three reasons: ordinarily
that their virtue be tried, sometimes that their soul may
be purified, now and then as punishment for their sins." [18]

122. From what has been said, we may conclude that
every temptation is purely internal or purely external or
mixed, that is, both internal and external. The purely interior is born of concupiscence or any of the human passions. The external comes from any other source outside
the soul, such as the devil, bad example, seduction, or
direct enticement to evil, the world in general. The mixed
temptation is an external temptation that meets a response
in human concupiscence, which becomes thereby an ally
and accomplice of the external tempter. In beginners and
in imperfect souls, practically every external temptation
becomes a mixed temptation because the passions are
unmortified and the appetites unruly and easily excited by
any external suggestion. In mortified and perfect souls,
there is usually no such reaction or answer from the side
of the internal enemy, and the temptation remains merely
external and, therefore, less dangerous.

D. RESISTANCE TO TEMPTATION

123. Every Christian must be convinced that he is
facing the enemy all his life and that sooner or later he
will be attacked. He must be prepared for the attack and

[17] *Vitae patrum,* I; *Vita Antonii,* 5; *Historia Lausiaca,* 23.
[18] *Collationes,* 6, 11.

not be taken by surprise. To this end he must watch and
pray: "Watch ye; and pray that ye enter not into temptation. The spirit indeed is willing, but the flesh is weak." [19]
The Apostle Peter experienced the truth of these words
soon after hearing them from our Lord's lips. Their meaning is that we must be always prepared. At the first onset
of temptation we must reject it immediately without any
hesitation. Whoever hesitates through curiosity gives signs
of surrender. Hesitation is the beginning of defeat. Such
was the case with Eve. On the other hand we have the
example of Christ in the desert.[20] To every suggestion
of the devil, Christ at once replied with the manifest will
of God, against which the temptation was directed. The
known will of God is the supreme rule of our conduct.
Any invitation to abandon it is an incitement to revolt
and to sin; it is the enemy of God attacking God's citadel
on earth, the human soul. There can be no idle conversation or trafficking with the enemy; there must be absolute
and disdainful refusal. At the same time, we must have
recourse to prayer; we must turn to God with humility
and confidence, and never cease praying until the enemy
has been put to flight and the waves of the stormy sea
have subsided.

124. Resistance to temptation is either active or passive. Active resistance is a direct counteraction of the
will, which expresses itself in the firm resolution to do
the will of God and not that of his enemy, and positive
acts of the contrary virtue, e.g., conquering impatience
with patience, anger with meekness, sensuality with mortification.

---

[19] Matt. 26:41.
[20] Matt. 4:1–11.

Passive resistance consists simply in brushing aside the evil suggestion by turning the attention to something else. This passive behavior is particularly recommended in temptations of a delicate nature, whereby the attempt to offer positive resistance may add fuel to the fire of temptation. Such is the case with temptations against faith, charity, chastity. The same procedure should be adopted against all temptations arising from representations of the imagination. The imagination is like a group of actors or minstrels, whose acting is encouraged by the attention of the audience; if nobody pays any attention, their acting is soon over.[21]

125. After the temptation has passed, if a reasonable doubt remains whether there has been any consent, we should not try to review or analyze the whole course of the temptation in order to determine the degree of the will's participation. This would be equivalent to inviting the temptation to return and would only make the situation worse if not desperate. The principles set forth in the beginning of this chapter regarding the nature of temptation should prove helpful in removing doubt and anxiety. The sin is in the will, not in feelings of the lower nature, much less in the imagination. But a doubtful mind, after temptation, has often the effect of humbling and purifying the soul. Besides, the violence of temptation may make us think that we have wandered far away from God, or that God has abandoned us to the enemy or to our reprobate senses. Nothing is more false. No matter how vile the temptation, the Master is closer at hand to His disciple than at any other time, just as the valiant general is closer to his soldiers during an attack of the enemy

[21] T. Pesch, S.J., *Christliche Lebensphilosophie*, chap. 113.

than at any other time. St. Athanasius, in his *Life of St. Anthony*, relates that, after one of those long and dreadful temptations sustained by St. Anthony, when calm had returned and the Lord comforted the saint with a vision, Anthony asked: "Where have you been? Why did you not appear from the beginning in order to relieve my pains?" Then he heard a voice saying: "I was here, Anthony, and I was waiting, watching your fight. Therefore, on account of your resistance and your victory, I will always be your helper and I will make your name celebrated in the whole world." [22]

E. The Particular Examination

126. Among the active means of spiritual purgation, the examination of conscience holds a most important place. The examination of conscience may be general or particular. The object of the first is to discover all the faults committed. The particular examination has a single point for its object, either one fault we have resolved to correct, or one virtue we intend to acquire. The general examination of thoughts, words, and deeds of commission and omission during the entire day, must be followed by an act of thanksgiving for graces received and of sorrow for sins committed. An examination of conscience often forms part of our mental prayer when we examine our conduct in the light of the truth just contemplated, to discover whether we have lived up to it or not. The object of general examination is to purge our conscience of sins that have been committed.

127. The object of the particular examination is the rooting out of one particular vice or fault and the planting

[22] *Vita S. Antonii.* 10.

of one particular virtue. The great utility of this exercise was known not only to spiritual writers of old,[23] but also to less spiritual persons who longed for moral perfection; e.g., Benjamin Franklin, who describes at length the method of a particular examination he followed for a while when he had "conceived the bold and arduous project of arriving at moral perfection. I wished to live without committing any fault at any time, and to conquer all that either natural inclination, custom, or company might lead me into."[24]

St. Ignatius [25] gives the following rules for the particular examination:

In the morning, on rising, resolve to avoid this sin or defect. Toward noon ask God that He may grant you to remember how often you have fallen into it and to avoid it in the future. Then examine, thinking over the time passed since your rising to this time, the number of faults committed, marking them by so many points in the first line of a figure like the following:

Days of the Week

1st day	✿
2d day	✿
3d day	✿
4th day	✿
5th day	✿
6th day	✿
7th day	✿

This done, renew your resolutions for the rest of the day. In the evening, after supper, make a new examination like the first, mark-

[23] Cassian, *Collationes*, 5, 27; St. Athanasius, *Vita S. Antonii*, 55; Origen, *Hom. in Cant.*, 2, 8.
[24] *Autobiography*, chap. 6.
[25] *Spiritual Exercises*, Part II.

ing the faults on the second line.[26] At each fault against the resolutions taken, put your hand on your heart and repent of your fall. This may be done without being noticed. At night count the points of the two examinations, and see whether from the first to the second you have made any amendment. Compare in the same way the day or the week which is ending with the preceding day or week. . . . The subject of the particular examination should be ordinarily the predominant passion, that is, the one that is the source of the greatest number of the faults that you commit and that consequently is the great obstacle to your sanctification. This examination on the predominant passion should be continued until it is entirely overcome, or at least notably weakened.[27]

128. To remain faithful to such a method of particular examination for a long time, is a sign of self-discipline and mortification. The continual practice, with the help of divine grace, and the other spiritual means of meditation, self-denial, and the like, will ultimately be instrumental in uprooting the capital vices and the predominant passions of the soul and in preparing the ground for the planting of solid virtues, which is the task of the illuminative way.

[26] In the original, St. Ignatius has two lines for each day of the week.
[27] *Spiritual Exercises*, pp. 255 ff.

CHAPTER X

THE ILLUMINATIVE WAY

"I am the light of the world: he that followeth Me, walketh not in darkness, but shall have the light of life" (John 8:12).

A. DEFINITION

129. The term "illuminative way" is derived from *lumen* ("light"). The state of sin is the state of spiritual death, symbolized by darkness. Sinners are "those that sit in darkness, and in the shadow of death." [1] The grace of God gives life to the sinner, and with life he sees the light of day. In the first stage of the spiritual life, the purgative way, that light is usually clouded and obscured by the lingering shadows of past sins, bad habits not yet overcome, frequent and violent temptations, doubts. It is the gray light of early morning. In the illuminative way we have full daylight, a light that no passing cloud or occasional shadow can obscure. It is the daylight that streams down from heaven, from the Sun of justice into the soul. Light gives a sense of peace, safety, and security to travelers. The same sense of peace and security is felt by those who travel on the way of perfection and have reached this second stage of the road. During the purgative way they were dominated mostly by fear; in the illuminative way they are governed by hope; those who have reached the unitive way are guided by love.

[1] Luke 1:79.

130. Souls in the illuminative way are so advanced that they easily avoid mortal sins and strive sincerely to acquire solid virtues, but they are still susceptible to venial sins, which they frequently commit. They are not yet perfect but they are making progress on the way of perfection. They have overcome their unruly passions and evil habits and have scored many victories over the enemies of their salvation through self-denial, by resisting temptations, by perpetual watching and praying; hence the easiness in overcoming mortal sin. It is especially in this last point that they differ from those in the purgative way, where it is still difficult to avoid mortal sin altogether. Another characteristic sign of this way is the fact that in mental prayer the action of the will prevails over consideration. This condition brings about another form of mental prayer, which is proper to the illuminative way and is called the affective prayer. In addition, temptations in general are overcome more easily. The soul feels detached from all worldly vanities and is more recollected, enjoying longer periods of peace and spiritual consolation. It strives to avoid not only mortal sins but also deliberate venial sins, although not always successful with regard to the latter.

131. In the purgative way the soul's principal aim was to purge itself from sin; in the illuminative way its main purpose is to adorn itself with virtues. This is done by imitating the example of Christ, whose life constitutes the ordinary subject of meditation during this period. Since He is "the light of the world," the more the soul advances in knowledge of Him and in grace, so will the splendors of His light increase on the soul's way to perfection and holiness.

This stage of the spiritual life is sometimes called the state of devout souls. It is to be highly esteemed because very meritorious, although not perfect. Many souls remain all their lives in this state without advancing any farther, either for lack of zeal and fervor or for lack of guidance and instruction.

In addition to all other means of perfection already explained, we must now turn our attention to those that are peculiar to the illuminative way. These are affective prayer and the acquisition of Christian virtues.

B. AFFECTIVE PRAYER

132. Affective prayer takes its name from the word *affectus* ("affections"). It is that form of mental prayer in which the affection of the heart (and the will) have a much larger share than the considerations of the intellect. One attains to this form of prayer ordinarily after a long and diligent practice of meditation. When the intellect has often considered the various mysteries of religion from every angle and when their truth and beauty are deeply impressed in the mind through meditation, it happens that as soon as any such mystery is called to mind, immediately and without any reasoning of the intellect the heart and the will are stirred by love and other affections, so that these occupy practically all the time spent in mental prayer. Balthasar Alvarez considers this method of prayer the one most used.

133. With this form of prayer we pass from the philosophical to the mystical method, where love takes the place of understanding, although all understanding is not excluded, because love is impossible without it, but most of the understanding is done by love. It is the beginning of the *amo ut intelligam* of the mystics. When we use the word "mystic" in connection with an ascetic form of prayer, we take that word in a broad sense. We are still far from the form of prayer that is strictly mystical. When love begins to dispense with the fastidious reasoning of the mind, we have the love that surpasses intelligence. It is interesting and relevant to note what J. J. Surin writes.

Love surpasses intelligence when man strives to come to God by way of his affections rather than by reasoning powers. It is certain that this way is more pleasing to God than the way of speculation, however enlightened. Pico della Mirandola, the quantity of whose teaching exceeded its quality, says, after having written much: "It is very silly to take so much trouble to come to the sovereign Good by means of study when assuredly He can be reached quicker by way of affections; with less trouble too, for nothing is so easy as to love." St. Ignatius recommends this path to his religious, to whom he assigned a year after their studies for a more perfect approach to God: this period is called *schola affectus,* a school of affection. . . .

True devotion does not consist in reasoning and speculation and a great deal of brain work, but in submission and humility of the heart which, being joined with love, not only unites the heart with God, but brings as well a great enlightening, for divine love is a clear fire from which men receive great abundance of exalted thoughts: so much so that it is a great mistake to encumber the mind with one's efforts to teach it too much. Love is an easy-flowing river which carries treasures of understanding and knowledge gently to the soul.[2]

134. We do not agree with Abbé A. Saudreau, when he says: "We class with affective prayer the prayer of supernatural recollection which St. Teresa refers to.[3] It is a well known fact that, only from the Fourth Mansion

---

[2] *Fondements de la vie spirituel,* V, 9.

[3] *Fourth Mansion,* chap. 3. *The Degrees of Spiritual Life,* Vol. I, Part III, chap. 1.

on, St. Teresa explains purely mystical forms of prayer. The word 'supernatural' in her language stands for supernatural *quoad rem* and *quoad modum*. It describes infused forms of prayers and it stands in place of the word 'mystic,' taken in its restricted meaning. This meaning is evident from her own description and explanation:

"The first prayer that I felt, in my judgment, to be supernatural—so I call that which no skill or effort of ours, however much we labor, can attain to, though we should prepare ourselves for it, and that preparation must be of great service—is an interior recollection that is felt in the soul." [4]

"This is something supernatural, which we cannot acquire by all our diligence, because it is a settling of the soul in peace; or rather, to speak more correctly, our Lord leads her into peace by His presence." [5]

It appears from these words that the "prayer of supernatural recollection" is nothing but the prayer of quiet, or the prayer of passive recollection, which is infused and purely mystical. The affective prayer is an ascetical form of prayer and a common one. The mystical element of love and affection enters into it, but it is the result of our diligence aided by ordinary grace; it is active form of mental prayer and it may be called mystical only in a broad sense. Confusion results when ascetical and mystical forms of prayer are not distinguished from each other.

135. Although St. Theresa and other spiritual writers of her time do not employ the term "affective prayer," this form of prayer was well known to them. A mental prayer consisting for the most part of affections, based on a simple

[4] *Relation*, p. 5.
[5] *The Way of Perfection*, p. 31.

thought or idea and without considerations, was known to every saint and, we may say, to every pious soul. This is what St. Theresa tells of herself, when she had not yet received the grace of mystical contemplation. She says:

> This was my method of prayer: as I could not make reflections with my mind, I tried to picture Christ as within me. . . . I did many simple things of this kind; and in particular I used to find myself most at home in the prayer in the Garden, whither I went in His company. I thought of the bloody sweat, and of the affliction He endured there; I wished, if it had been possible, to wipe away the painful sweat from His face. . . . For my part, I believe that my soul gained very much in this way, because I began to practice prayer without knowing what it was.[6]

136. Among the various forms of mental prayer described by St. Ignatius in his *Spiritual Exercises*, there are some that closely resemble the affective prayer; these are (1) contemplation of persons, words, and actions of a mystery or event; (2) the application of the senses; (3) the meditated vocal prayer. In all these forms of prayer the action of the mind is reduced and that of the affections is increased.

These various methods are less fatiguing than the discursive meditation. To affective prayer belongs also the so-called method of St. Sulpice, mentioned elsewhere, which is better adapted to souls advanced in the illuminative way than to beginners.

137. In all these various forms of affective prayer the same rules of remote and proximate preparation must be observed. Preparatory prayer and preludes open the exercise, and it is closed with colloquies. Here, too, a

---

[6] *Life*, 9.

special fruit must be derived besides the general one, and a practical resolution must be taken, as we pointed out in speaking of meditation.

We must note here that, when St. Ignatius speaks of contemplation of persons, words, and actions, he takes the term "contemplation" in a very broad sense. It has nothing to do with acquired contemplation and much less with infused contemplation. It means only that the persons on whom we are meditating, together with their words and actions, must become, as it were, alive while we look attentively and lovingly at them and at what they do, and listen to what they actually say or might say. The simple gaze of contemplation is followed by various affections and salutary resolutions. This form of prayer is best adapted for the mysteries of the life and death of our Savior.

The application of the senses is an easy and simple form of prayer, in which each of our senses is applied in turn to the subject, usually a biblical fact or some other concrete mystery of religion. After the application of each sense, corresponding affections and resolutions follow.

The meditated vocal prayer consists in taking an ordinary vocal prayer, like the Our Father, and considering briefly and lovingly each word in succession, long enough to stir the affections of the heart and inspire opportune practical resolutions, concluding by simply reciting devoutly the rest of the words not considered. "If a single word of the prayer we are reciting in this way suffices to occupy the mind and the heart all the time destined to prayer, we must put off to another day the meditation of the rest." [7]

[7] St. Ignatius, *Spiritual Exercises.*

138. Hugh of Palma [8] says of the illuminative way that
in it the mind by reflection is kindled unto love and that
in meditating upon the Lord's Prayer and seeking for the
mystical sense in Sacred Scripture the soul will rise to the
love of God. It must be noted, however, that it is not the
subject or the form of mental prayer but the subjective
disposition of the soul that causes affective prayer and
gives it a specific form. This subjective disposition is
brought about by spiritual illumination, which in turn
is the fruit of the long and continual exercise of discursive
mental prayer, as stated above.

St. Theresa seems to speak of this kind of prayer when
she writes: "I did all I could to imagine Jesus Christ, our
God and our Lord, present within me. And this was the
way I prayed. If I meditated on any mystery of His life,
I represented it to myself as within me, though the greater
part of my time I spent in reading good books, which was
all my comfort." [9] In another instance the same St. Theresa
considers the advantage of meditated vocal prayer and
calls it a prayer of recollection. This is active recollection,
to be distinguished from the supernatural mentioned
above, which is infused and passive and therefore mystical. St. Theresa says:

In order that you may not think little advantage is gained by
praying vocally with perfection, I tell you it is very possible that,
while you are repeating the Our Father or saying some other vocal
prayer, our Lord may raise you to perfect contemplation. . . .

Consider what St. Augustine says, that he sought God in many
places, and came at last to find him in himself. Do you think it is
of little importance for a distracted soul to understand this truth,
and to know that she need not go to heaven to speak with the Eter-

[8] Prologue to his *Mystica theologia.*
[9] *Life,* chap. 4.

nal Father, or to regale herself with him? Nor need she speak aloud, for however low she may speak, he is so near, that he will hear us; neither does she require wings to fly and seek him, but she can compose herself in solitude and behold him within herself: and let her not separate from so good a guest, but with great humility speak to him as a Father, entreat him as a Father, relate her troubles to him, and beg a remedy for them, knowing that she is not worthy to be his daughter. . . . This kind of prayer, though it be vocal, recollects the understanding much sooner, and is a prayer of recollection, because in it the soul recollects all the faculties and enters within herself with her God.[10]

139. This recollection is an active one because it is not the result of an exterior cause; "in it the soul recollects all the faculties." It is the equivalent of affective prayer. It sometimes happens that souls are raised to the prayer of quiet and of infused contemplation after spending more or less time in this exercise. This seems to have been the case with St. Theresa herself.[11] From this fact many authors have concluded that the mystical life begins toward the end of the illuminative life. Nothing could be more incorrect. The mystical life can begin any time God wills it to. Divine grace may dispense with the ordinary purgative and illuminative way or reduce them to a minimum, as seems to have been the case with St. Paul. St. Theresa describes her own personal experiences, as she tells many times in her writings, and does not explain what generally happens to other souls.

After the affective prayer, we have another form of active mental prayer, called acquired contemplation, which is the prayer proper to the unitive way, as we will explain in a future chapter.

[10] *The Way of Perfection,* 25, 28.
[11] *Life,* chaps. 4, 10.

140. In affective prayer more than in meditation, spiritual consolations and delights are experienced. One should accept them humbly and gratefully from God because they are given for our spiritual advancement. Their purpose is to purify and detach our sensible faculties from their disorderly tendencies and to encourage the soul to be constant and to persevere on the way to perfection. It is an old maxim, common among ancient spiritual writers (St. Dorotheus, for example), that whatever the spirit does not joyfully embrace cannot be of a long duration. In spiritual life one meets with duties that have no charm for the soul; their performance necessitates a kind of violence but *nihil violentum stabile* ("that which is violent cannot endure"); therefore the necessity of something that makes the spiritual life delightful and attractive above everything else in the world. Spiritual consolations are not to be regarded superciliously as mere "sweets," good only for children in spiritual life, because sturdy adults also need them occasionally. Father Libermann in his *Spiritual Writings* thus describes the effects of spiritual consolations:

God disposes the sensible faculties so that they lend themselves to His merciful designs by way of sweetness, enjoyment, and satisfaction. These starved faculties, which have been filled with the corruptions of the creature, begin to see that in God alone their true good is to be found. They begin to break with creatures and learn to seek refuge in God. This purifies them from the carnal desire for the creature. They are content; they enjoy God; they love to take their pleasure in Him alone.

All the considerations of the intellect, all the convincing proofs of the learned, will not be strong enough to establish the soul in God and in the practice of virtue until the heart has been touched and penetrated. The reasons of the heart are the most convincing. Once the heart has been surrendered to God and to His cause, nothing on earth can stop it on the way of perfection. After such complete surrender, when it has already "tasted and seen how sweet the Lord is," the soul can work and suffer for a long time without spiritual consolations, knowing well that one day the good Lord will be its reward.

CHAPTER XI

PRACTICE AND ACQUISITION OF VIRTUES

A. DEFINITION

141. The nature of virtues, their classification, and the obligation to acquire them are fully explained in moral theology, and such a knowledge is here presupposed. They are considered here only as a specific means of Christian perfection. It is no longer a question of what kind of sin one commits in transgressing this or that virtue but rather of how to acquire the habit of virtue and how to practice it to a high degree of perfection, even to a heroic degree.

According to Cassiodorus, "virtue has its name from freshness (*a viriditate*) because no labor makes it grow languid." [1] Its meanings are many, but one element is common to them all, and that is vigor, power. Not excluding the etymology given by Cassiodorus, it seems rather that the ultimate root of the word is *vir* ("man") or *vis* ("strength"), meaning, therefore, a manly quality of vigor and strength. When taken in the physical sense, it means courage, valor. Here we take the word in its moral sense; thus it was defined by St. Augustine as that "good quality of the mind, by which we live right and of which nobody makes a bad use." [2] According to Aristotle, "virtue is the disposition of what is perfect to what is excellent." [3] The

---

[1] *Sup. Psalm.* 139:8.
[2] *De lib. arbit.*, II, 19.
[3] *Physic.*, VII.

same Aristotle, after demonstrating that virtues are neither feelings nor capacities, concludes that they must be a state or habit: "Virtue must be a state whereby man comes to be good and whereby he will perform well his proper work." [4] Sporadic good actions do not make a man virtuous; virtue does not consist in a good act but in a good habit. The act is the fruit; virtue is the branch. Good habits of virtue either are infused or are acquired by a long and frequent repetition of good actions. A virtue is infused when that good quality or disposition of our faculties does not arise from a repetition of acts or by merely natural efforts, but is given by God. It is a proximate principle of supernatural activity in the soul, the remote principle being sanctifying grace. By means of such infused principles, supernatural acts are made possible, but it does not follow that they are made easy, although the inclination to the good that they involve removes some of the difficulty. Infused virtue may be either theological (faith, hope, charity) or moral (prudence, justice, fortitude, and temperance). The latter are the cardinal virtues, under which all the other moral virtues are grouped: e.g., patience is a species of fortitude; obedience a species of justice; chastity, humility, and meekness are three different species of temperance; counsel and discretion are two moral virtues belonging to prudence.

142. Moral virtues are either acquired by practice, that is, the repetition of suitable acts, with or without the supernatural help of grace, or they are immediately infused by God along with sanctifying grace. The infused virtue does not make a man virtuous but gives him the possibility of practicing virtue in the supernatural order;

[4] *Ethic.*, II.

he has merely a new operative principle of supernatural activity in his soul. He must cooperate with divine grace and act in accordance with such infused principles or virtues in order to acquire solid virtue. The infused virtues are like the "talents" [5] which the nobleman of the parable gave his servants, saying: "Trade till I come." [6] The servant who kept his "talent" idle is called a "wicked servant" and is punished for his inactivity. Operative principles of a supernatural order were infused in our souls that they be put to work and produce supernatural acts.

143. It is of such acts that we treat here, namely, the practice of supernatural virtues, but without excluding natural virtues. "Human virtue, which is the principle of all the good acts of man, consists in following the rule of human acts, which is twofold, . . . viz., human reason and God." [7]

In the practice of the various moral virtues, we must remember that "no strictly true virtue is possible without charity." [8] The reason is that virtue is ordered to man's good; now, man's ultimate and principal good is God; and to this good, man is ordered by charity. Man's secondary or particular good may be twofold: that is, truly good in itself and ordered to the principal good (God), or only apparently good, deviating from the principal good (God). Hence only true virtue leads man to God, and no true virtue is possible without charity. We may speak of a virtue directed to some particular end where there is no charity involved. But if that particular end is only an apparent good, then that virtue is not true, but false and

[5] Matt. 25:14 ff.; Luke 19:12 ff.
[6] Luke 19:13.
[7] St. Thomas, *Summa theol.*, IIa IIae, q.23, a.3.
[8] *Ibid.*, a.7.

counterfeit. Such counterfeits are mentioned by St. Augustine:

> The prudence of the miser, whereby he devises various roads to gain, is no true virtue; nor the miser's justice, whereby he scorns the property of another through fear of severe punishment; nor the miser's temperance, whereby he curbs his desire for expensive pleasures; nor the miser's fortitude, whereby as Horace says,[9] "he braves the sea, he crosses mountains, he goes through fire in order to avoid poverty."[10]

When the particular good is a true good, then the virtue will be a true virtue but imperfect unless it is referred to God, the final and perfect good. So, for example, working for the welfare of the family or society, is an act of a true virtue but remains imperfect if not referred to God, to whom all the particular goods of the individual, the family, and the state must be subordinated.

144. All supernatural virtues receive their form from charity; charity is not only the queen of virtues but their very soul and life, because it is "charity which directs the acts of all other virtues to the last end."[11] Any act of any moral virtue that is not animated by charity explicitly or implicitly cannot be called supernatural and is not to be considered an expression of Christian life and perfection, even though it may be an act of natural virtue. These conclusions are based on the words of St. Paul: "If I should distribute all my goods to the poor, and if I should deliver my body to be burned, and have not charity, it profiteth me nothing."[12]

[9] *Epist.*, I, 45.
[10] *Contra Iulianum*, IV, 3.
[11] St. Thomas, *Summa theol.*, IIa IIae, q.23, a.8.
[12] I Cor. 13:3.

b. Dynamic Motives and Virtues

145. The reason why we speak of virtue in the illuminative way is mainly this: in the illuminative way one of the great obstacles in the practice of virtue has been overcome. This great obstacle is the inertia of the will. Lack of knowledge is much less an impediment in the practice of virtue than lack of good will. In affective prayer the heart has been touched, the fire of love has been kindled, and fire is one of the commonest sources of dynamic power in both the physical and the moral order, in the mechanical and psychological world. Faith, hope, and love are the highest motives in arousing the human will to action. To such motives a dynamic or motor idea should be added in order to stir the will with alacrity. The pious and deep affections experienced in affective prayer should be the dynamo of virtue.

Another energizing source of virtue is the example of our Lord, His Blessed Mother, and our patron saints. The contemplation of virtue, not as an abstraction but as a historic fact in the lives of persons we love and esteem renders it more desirable, for we are moved to imitate them. Therefore also the life of Christ is the ordinary subject of mental prayer in the illuminative way.

The more the habit of virtue takes root in the soul the more easily do all the faculties of the soul surrender to God, the soul itself passes into the service of God, and God's kingdom is established in the soul.

Every person has certain natural dispositions that constitute his personal temperament. Among these there is generally one dominant natural virtue which, if perfected by grace, can become the foundation of sanctity, just as

among the same traits of character there is a dominant
fault which if not checked will dispose to sin and spiritual ruin. It is these characteristic virtues and faults that
determine the individuality of a saint or a sinner. It is important to know both and to make them the subject of
the particular examination.

146. Christian perfection requires solid virtues, that
is, virtues that are firm, deep-rooted, and unshakable.
Perfect sanctity demands heroic virtues. Heroic virtues
consist in the habitual practice of all the virtues both theological and cardinal (moral), in the highest degree and
under most difficult circumstances. These are the virtues
of the Christian heroes, the saints. This heroism is found
not only in the martyrs but in all other saints as well. It
is the essential criterion for the canonization of the servants of God.[13] To be heroically virtuous a person must
practice all the virtues; he may not exclude any virtue,
for if he sins against one virtue alone, no matter how
perfect he may be in his observance of all the others,
there can be no question of heroism: *Bonum ex integra
causa.*

147. We mention heroic virtue here for the sake of
completeness, not because we should expect anyone in
the illuminative way to practice it. Heroic acts of virtue
may be performed at any time, even in the purgative way,
but they remain isolated and are not to be confused with
the permanent habit of the soul bent upon heroism in the
practice of virtue. Those acts are heroic *per modum actus*
but not *per modum habitus.* In the spiritual life the proper
place for heroic virtue is the unitive way.

[13] Benedict XIV, *De beatificatione servorum Dei et de beatorum canonizatione,* Bk. III.

148. Virtue is the child of prayer and mortification: "Prayer, too, is a virtue, although it is the mother of them all because it begets them through its affinity with Christ." [14] Without self-denial and mortification there can be no true virtue, and surely no heroic virtue. As a matter of fact, if during a person's process of beatification it becomes evident that he did not suffer trials and practice bodily penances and mortification, the whole process concerning his heroic virtues is to be shelved.[15] Virtue that is not built by hardships must be looked upon with suspicion:

Jesus Christ, who has anointed you with his Spirit, and taken you to the arena, has seen it good, before the day of conflict, to take you from a condition more pleasant in itself, and has imposed on you a harder treatment, that your strength might be greater. For the athletes, too, are set apart to a more stringent discipline, that they may have their physical power built up. They are kept from luxury, from daintier meats, from more pleasant drinks; they are pressed, racked, worn out; the harder their labors in the preparatory training, the stronger is the hope of victory. "And they," says the Apostle, "that they may obtain a corruptible crown." We, with the eternal crown in our mind, look upon the prison as our training-ground, that at the end of final judgment we may be brought forth well disciplined by many trials; since virtue is built up by hardships, as by voluptuous indulgence it is overthrown.[16]

This was commonly the language of the Fathers to the confessors of the faith preparing for the final struggle, their exhortation to heroism in Christian virtue.

[14] Mark the Hermit, *Concerning those who think to be justified through works,* 33.
[15] Benedict IV, *op. cit.,* Bk. III, 28.
[16] Tertullian, *Ad martyres,* 3.

C. Temptations in the Illuminative Way

149. Temptations are not limited to the purgative way
or to any one period in the spiritual life. Sometimes it happens that those more advanced in virtue experience
longer and more violent temptations than beginners. This
should not surprise them and much less cause them to
be discouraged. We are warned of such an eventuality by
our Lord Himself, who said: "When an unclean spirit is
gone out of a man, he walketh through dry places seeking
rest, and findeth none. Then he saith: I will return into
my house from whence I came out. And coming he findeth it empty, swept, and garnished. Then he goeth, and
taketh with him seven other spirits more wicked than
himself; and they enter in and dwell there: and the last
state of that man is made worse than the first." [17]
The "house" that is "empty, swept, and garnished" is the
soul that is free from sin and adorned with virtues; it is
the Christian soul in the illuminative way. The old
temptations would prove powerless in this state, hence
the tempter goes in search of an alliance with other more
wicked enemies of the soul. Their sevenfold assault,
which reminds us of the seven capital sins, is terrifying
and, if the soul is not firmly established in charity, it will
fall miserably. These are the trials of virtue; these are the
storms that require deep roots in every spiritual plant
to resist the storm; this is the training school of Christian
heroes. The violence of the temptation is in proportion to
our inner virtue and perfection, because we have the as-
surance that God does not permit us to be tempted above

[17] Matt. 12:43–45.

our strength; hence it is a sign that we have made some progress in virtue if we are tempted more assiduously now than at the beginning of our spiritual life. Strong temptations require the exercise of strong virtues and thereby they offer opportunity for great merits. For such reasons as these, temptations occur also in the unitive way and even after the celestial experience of a mystical union, as was the case with St. Paul after he had been caught up to the third heaven: "And lest the greatness of the revelations should exalt me, there was given me a sting of my flesh, an angel of Satan to buffet me. For which thing thrice I besought the Lord, that it might depart from me. And He said to me: My grace is sufficient for thee: for power (*virtus*) is made perfect in infirmity." [18]

D. Tepidity

150. Tepidity or lukewarmness is one of the most subtle and insidious infections of spiritual life. It is not a specific sin or temptation but an attitude that endangers the whole spiritual life, stops all progress in virtue, and undermines the whole structure of Christian perfection. As the name implies, it is a lack of fervor, a spiritual languor, a slow-working disease, that has been compared to the continual low fever of the consumptives. It means not only spiritual inactivity but spiritual indolence, a form of sluggishness *sui generis* that, if not checked, leads to spiritual death.

151. This obstacle or spiritual malady may be encountered at any stage in the way of perfection; beginners and perfect souls may be affected by tepidity, but those in the illuminative way seem to be the more exposed to it than

[18] II Cor. 12:7-9.

the rest. This is one of the common reasons why so many who have enthusiastically entered the way of perfection fall along the road and lie by the wayside, road-weary and far from the goal. This is the main cause of so many unfinished saints.

152. Tepidity is essentially spiritual languor. We must learn the cause and eliminate it. In spiritual life, as in the physical life, weakness and languor are the effect either of undernourishment or of some dangerous microbe that has entered the organism and is undermining resistance. Neglect of mental prayer, mortification, and recollection and, above all, of devout reception of Holy Communion, causes spiritual undernourishment. Dalliance with our dominant passion or pet fault is equivalent to fostering an infection.

The only remedy is to eliminate the cause and effect a spiritual cure with the means already described. Tepidity usually begins with the neglect of little things, small duties, until such omissions become habitual and pave the way for the neglect and contempt of the greater things and grave obligations: *Qui spernit modica, paulatim decidet.* A good preventive, therefore, is the conscientious fulfillment of every duty no matter how small. Tepidity is a dangerous state for the soul because the rehabilitation of such a soul is often more difficult than the conversion of a sinner. It is a condition that is loathsome in the eyes of the Lord. We read in the Apocalypse: "I know thy works, that thou art neither cold nor hot. . . . I will begin to vomit thee out of my mouth. Because thou sayest: I am rich and made wealthy, and have need of nothing: and knowest not that thou art wretched and miserable and poor and blind and naked. I counsel thee to buy of me gold fire tried, that thou mayest be made rich and mayest be clothed in white garments, and that the shame of thy nakedness may not appear. And anoint thy eyes with eyesalve, that thou mayest see." [19] Here not only is the wretched condition of the tepid soul described, but the remedies are indicated: the pure "gold" of charity and the "eyesalve" of mental prayer.

[19] Apoc. 3:15–18.

CHAPTER XII

THE UNITIVE WAY

"I in them, and Thou in Me; that they may be made perfect in one" (John 17:23).

We introduce the subject of the present chapter with the following excerpts from St. Catherine of Siena and from Richard Rolle.

I do not act in like manner with those most perfect ones who have attained great perfection and are entirely dead to their own wills. I remain continually both by grace and by feeling in their soul, so that at any time that they wish they can unite their mind to me through love. They can in no way be separated from my love, for by love they arrived at so close a union. Every place is to them an oratory, every moment a time for prayer—their conversation has ascended from earth to heaven—that is to say, they have cut off from themselves every form of earthly affection and sensual self-love, and have risen above themselves into the height of heaven, having climbed the ladder of virtues and mounted the three steps which I figured to thee, in the body of my Son.[1]

O sweet and delectable light, that is my infinite Maker, enlighten the face and the vision of my inward eye with uncreated charity, and kindle my mind with thy savour, that, thoroughly cleansed from uncleanness and made marvelous with thy gifts, it may swiftly fly to the high mirth of love; that I may sit and rest in thee, Jesus, rejoicing and going as it were, ravished with heavenly sweetness; and that, established in the beholding of heavenly things, I shall never be glad but in Divine things.[2]

[1] St. Catherine of Siena, *Dialogue.*
[2] Richard Rolle, *The Amending of Life,* chap. 11.

A. Definition

153. The unitive way is the way of the perfect souls. We have already noted the meaning of "perfection" and "perfect." The word "perfect" implies here only a relative and progressive perfection, not an absolute one. It is not a state but a way of perfection, the final stretch of road. Since the unitive way arrives at the goal, it is characterized by a certain stability that could not be expected in the other two. This stability which, however, is only relative, is the result of perfect self-control acquired through self-denial and mortification, of the deep-rooted habits of virtue and especially of perfect charity. The actions of a perfect soul know no wavering or hesitation. Except for common venial sins of fragility, generally not deliberate, nothing mars their path of virtue and holiness. Because of a certain uniformity and constancy in acting according to the Christian ideal of perfection, the unitive way may be called a state in the broad sense of the term, but it is a relative state only, for the possibility of sin is never precluded in the present life nor is the degree of perfection of charity and of the other virtues absolute.

This way is called unitive because it is the consummation of the others and because the soul is no longer governed by fear or hope, but by love. Love tends to union and is the consummation of that union. Hope looks to the expected good; love reaches it and rests in it. Yet that rest in the union with the desired good is not inactivity, because love can never be idle; rather it is life in its full meaning and most perfect form. This is the life of the saints, of the great Christian heroes whose deeds have astounded the world. Union here means union with God through love. It means also unification and simplification of the whole spiritual life, especially of the mode of prayer. Mastery means simplification, perfection. When we have acquired perfect mastery of an art, like the playing of an instrument, we find very simple what seemed to us extremely complicated and difficult in the beginning. Perfection, therefore, means simplicity; in fact, simplicity is one of the attributes of God, who is infinitely perfect.

154. Several authors speak of the unitive way as if it were the beginning of the mystical life. The same authors consider only one kind of contemplation, mystical and infused contemplation. Since the prayer proper to the unitive way is contemplation, they conclude that every contemplative is a mystic. We must make a distinction to avoid great confusion in theory and practice. We hold that there are two unitive ways and two kinds of contemplation. There is an ascetical or ordinary unitive way and a mystical or extraordinary one. The proper prayer of the ascetical unitive way is acquired contemplation, whereas infused contemplation is the proper prayer of the mystical. We should note here again that the word "mystic" is taken in its restricted meaning, denoting infused prayer, divine attraction and illumination, in a word, a passive state. The ascetic unitive way is still an active state even though the activity is extremely easy and simplified because of the mastery acquired. Many saints were transferred into mystical contemplation immediately after meditation or affective prayer, as seems to have been the case with St. Theresa. This fact may have led certain authors (e.g., Saudreau, Arintero, Vallgornera, Garrigou-Lagrange, Louismet) to conclude that everything which

follows the illuminative way is mystical. St. Theresa in her works often insists on the fact that she is merely relating her own personal experiences, the ways in which God guided her soul and that she is not stating a general principle. As long as the soul keeps the initiative in prayer, its prayer is not mystical or extraordinary but ascetical or active, and its state is not a mystical state except in the sense that every prayer, every pious act, and hence the whole life of every good Christian, are mystical. This, in fact, is the meaning given the word "mystic" by Louismet.[3]

155. The unitive way comes closer to the mystical state than any of the preceding ways for more than one reason: the simplification of intellectual and affectional activity in mental prayer, the amenability of the soul to the inspirations and guidance of the Holy Ghost, and lastly the reign of love. These and other factors produce a striking similarity between the unitive way and mystical unions. But the similarity is only *quoad rem* and not *quoad modum;* the first is an active state, the second a passive one. It may happen that a mystical union, in the strict sense of the word, is granted during the ordinary, ascetical unitive way, but only transitorily, *per modum actus,* and for a very short time. Such an experience in itself alone would not change the nature of the unitive way. The first kind of unitive way, the ascetical, ordinary, or active, is explained here; the other, the mystical, extraordinary, or passive, is the subject of mystical theology.

156. The characteristic signs of the unitive way are evident from what has already been said. Having subjected the senses to reason, and the reason and heart to

[3] *The Mystical Life,* Pref.

God in the two preceding ways, the soul is more mani-
festly under the guidance of the Holy Ghost through infused gifts, the resistance and inertia of the will having
been conquered by charity. Mental prayer has been simplified also with regard to affections, and from affective
prayer it becomes acquired contemplation. The exercise
of prayer and of the presence of God becomes almost
uninterrupted. Interior peace is not easily disturbed even
in the midst of great trials. The zeal and fervor of the
spirit become a thirst for the salvation of souls and the
glory of God. The soul begins to enjoy already here on
earth the fruits of the Holy Ghost and the blessings promised in the beatitudes. This is a union which by virtue of
love tends to a kind of unity of the spirit with God: "That
they may be made perfect in one." [4] It is a unity of mind
and will sometimes found, though to a much lesser degree, even in natural human friendship.

In the supernatural order, a Christian knows that he is
a member of the mystical body of Christ: "Now you are
the body of Christ, and members of member." [5] This
union, which begins in baptism, is first realized now in all
its significance and importance.

B. ACQUIRED CONTEMPLATION

157. The term "contemplation" seems to be derived
originally from the common way of taking aim, in which
the weapon is held close to the temple (*con-temporatio,*
hence *contemplatio*): "*Quia sagittis praecipua contemplatione utantur*" (Pliny). It means generally a gazing
upon, a surveying, a very attentive consideration. It may

[4] John 17:23.
[5] I Cor. 12:27.

be purely mental or internal, or it may be both external (through the senses especially of sight and hearing) and internal. It is either natural or supernatural. Supernatural contemplation is either acquired or infused. Here we shall discuss only acquired contemplation.

158. Natural contemplation was well known to all great minds of the pagan world, philosophers, poets, and artists. Aristotle makes human happiness depend upon contemplation: "Human happiness goes as far as contemplation goes." According to Seneca: "That is true pleasure which is obtained by contemplation in a mind that is free from every stain and resplendent." For Cicero, contemplation is the natural food of the mind: "*Est [contemplatio] animorum ingeniorumque naturale quoddam quasi pabulum.*"

159. Supernatural contemplation, like the natural, consists subjectively in an absorbing interest in some thought or object that is continually occupying the mind and engrossing the affections. Objectively it is a religious truth or divine mystery which, through divine grace or a special divine illumination, elevates mind and heart to an absorbing knowledge and love of God.

Contemplation is a prayer in which the mind dispenses with reasoning and concentrates on God in simple gaze,[6] and with a simple wordless act of the will. Mental prayer has reached its perfection in all the soul's operations, its considerations and affections. In acquired contemplation this mastery is the fruit of a long practice of mental prayer, first with meditation and then with affective prayer. In infused contemplation such mastery and perfection is given by God directly. With acquired contemplation the

[6] St. Thomas, *Summa theol.*, IIa IIae, q. 180. a. 1.

soul reaches the ultimate term of the active and natural development of spiritual life. With infused contemplation the soul is introduced into the mystical union in the strict sense of the word.

c. Distinction between Acquired and Infused Contemplation

160. As already mentioned, several authors do not admit the existence of acquired contemplation; for them, every contemplation is infused. Thus Arintero, O.P., in *Verdadera mistica tradicional* (Salamanca, 1925); A. Saudreau, *The Degrees of the Spiritual Life* (London, 1926); E. Lamballe, *La contemplation* (Paris, 1916); E. Dimmler, *Beschauung und Seele* (Kempten, 1918); S. Louismet, *La contemplation chrétienne* (Paris, 1923); Garrigou-Lagrange, *Perfection et contemplation* (S. Maximin, 1923). The last mentioned theologian admits the possibility of acquired contemplation to a certain extent, but is more in favor of one form of contemplation.

161. In favor of an acquired contemplation, distinct from the infused contemplation, are the following theologians: J. de Guibert, S.J., *Theologia spiritualis ascetica et mystica* (Rome, 1939); Chrysogonus a Iesu Sacramentato, C.D., *Asceticae et mysticae summa* (Turin, 1936); Gabriele di S. M. Maddalena, *La mistica Teresiana* (Fiesole, 1935); A. Tanquerey, *The Spiritual Life* (Tournai, 1930); M. Grabmann, *Wesen und Grundlagen der kathol. Mystik* (Muenchen, 1922); A. Poulain, S.J., *The Graces of Interior Prayer* (St. Louis, Mo., 1910); Seisdedos, S.J., *Principios fundamentales de la mistica* (Madrid, 1913); Meynard, O.P., *Vie intérieure* (Paris, 3rd ed., 1899); and several others among the modern spiritual writers. It is sufficient to mention only one name among the classics of former days: J. B. Scaramelli, S.J., *Directorio mistico* (Venice, 1754). Scaramelli not only makes a distinction between the two kinds of contemplation but he also furnishes us with the best definition of acquired contemplation: "It is that contemplation which, with the aid of grace, we can acquire by our own endeavor, and particularly by a long practice of meditation; although, strictly speaking, it is not due to all these efforts" (Tr. 2, N. 69). The restriction made in the last part of the preceding definition is very important. When we speak of an active form of contemplation or of acquired contemplation, we do so with the understanding that in every supernatural mental prayer the soul depends on the help of divine grace; hence its activity includes some passivity. In acquired contemplation, the gifts of the Holy Ghost assist the soul in its heavenly ascent. Therefore, even though the natural elements of contemplation are acquired, the supernatural elements are infused. In spite of such infused and passive elements, the contemplation is still to be called acquired and active to distinguish it from that which is purely infused, toward which man cannot contribute anything positively but only negatively by simply removing the obstacles to the infusion of such grace. On the other hand, the passivity is not absolute in passive, infused contemplation because in receiving it the soul is moved to an *actio vitalis* of perception and love; it is not a dead mirror that reflects the ray of light without change; it adds, on the contrary, the human element to the divine light. Still the name is given always by the prevailing element.

162. Knowing the great and many blessings of contemplation, every soul tending to perfection is naturally interested to know whether we must simply expect it as a gratuitous gift from God or whether we may strive efficaciously to attain it, aided by ordinary grace. The reasons brought forward by the authors opposed to acquired contemplation seem to cast some doubt on its existence. Their reasons are as follows:

1. Acquired contemplation was unknown to the Fathers and to all spiritual writers before the seventeenth century. They know only infused contemplation. Besides, the idea of an acquired contemplation seems to have prepared the way for quietism and to have been condemned among the propositions of Molinos; e.g., "By acquired contemplation we arrive at a state in which we commit no kind of sin, neither mortal nor venial" (prop. 57).

2. Besides the *habitus fidei* which is sufficient for meditation, a new infused *habitus* seems to be required.

3. Even if such form of contemplation exists, it is only transitory as a connecting link between meditation and infused contemplation.

163. It is easy to answer these objections and prove positively the existence of acquired contemplation which is known also as the prayer of simplicity. It has been practiced from all times like meditation, but the explanation of it has evolved only gradually. As we have explained elsewhere, mental prayer was practiced always, but methodical mental prayer had its beginnings in the late Middle Ages. The fact that the Fathers and earlier writers did not employ the same terminology as we do does not prove anything. Two different ages may hold the same doctrine or truth but, in the natural development of the understanding of it, they may present that same doctrine in a form that is clearer and more specific at one time than at another.

The word *theoria* and *contemplatio* used by the Fathers had not only the meaning of infused contemplation, but also of other forms of contemplation: "Contemplation is sometimes taken strictly for the act of the intellect that meditates upon divine things. . . . Some other time, and commonly, for every act by which a person occupies himself with God alone after leaving behind all worldly business." [7] St. Bernard calls contemplation any perception of truth. Acquired contemplation is clearly indicated by Ricardus Victorinus in his *Beniamin maior* (V, 2): "The first way [of contemplating] is through human diligence; the third by divine grace only; the middle by the union of both human diligence and divine grace."

A little later, in the fifteenth century, we find Denis the Carthusian using the expression "acquired contemplation" in his *De fonte lucis* (c. 8). Thomas a Iesu, in his book *De contemplatione divina* (I, c. 2), proposes the distinction between acquired and infused contemplation with these words: "We call acquired that contemplation which we acquire by our own diligence and practice, not, however, without divine cooperation and grace; but we call infused that which comes from divine grace and inspiration only." This work appeared in 1620. The same author in a Spanish work published in 1609 says in the Preface that this word "acquired" was in use among the mystics of that period. Cardinal Brancati de Lauria, in his *De oratione Christiana* (Venice, 1687), proves that the Fathers of the Church were well acquainted with acquired contemplation, although they did not think of giv-

---

[7] St. Thomas, *IV Sent.* D. 15, q. 4, a. 1, qc2 ad 1.

ing it a special name, and that they therefore considered
it distinct from infused contemplation.

164. The Quietists of the seventeenth century understood acquired contemplation in their own distorted way,
according to their fundamental principle that all action
is an imperfection. They exclude all activity from acquired contemplation and make it a passive prayer;
whereas for us activity in its most perfect form is implied
in acquired contemplation. Another reason for the condemnation was the impeccability attributed by Molinos
to those who practice acquired contemplation. Everybody knows that no state of prayer, however sublime,
confers impeccability in this life.

165. Without any foundation, the authors of the contrary opinion advocate the necessity of a new infused
habitus besides the *habitus fidei* for any form of contemplation. This is denying that the soul can acquire a habit
by continual and diligent repetition of acts of an intellective and volitional order. In the ordinary and active form
of contemplation, the acquired habit, together with the
infused *habitus fidei*, divine grace and the infused gifts
of the Holy Ghost are sufficient.

166. Even if the acquired contemplation were of a
transitory nature only, there would be reason enough not
to confound it with infused contemplation. As a matter
of fact, acquired contemplation is no more transitory than
affective prayer, and even those who have occasionally
been favored with infused contemplation must, often and
for long periods of time, return to this form of acquired
contemplation, as St. Theresa affirms.[8] Many perfect souls
spend the rest of their lives in it. St. John of the Cross,

[8] *Moradas,* VI, 7.

without using the expression "acquired contemplation," describes it perfectly, calling it an acquired habit, resulting from the many acts of meditation, a habit that God sometimes produces in the soul independently of those acts:

> We must know that the purpose of meditation and mental discourse on divine things is to acquire some knowledge and love of God, and that every time the soul attains it through meditation we have one act; and just as in everything else repeated acts form habits in the soul, so the many acts of loving knowledge that the soul has derived . . . through a continued use become a habit in the soul itself. The very same thing, however, God accomplishes at times in many souls without need of any such acts (at least without a sufficient number of them) by placing them in contemplation without delay.[9]

167. Contemplation is *simplex intuitus veritatis* ("simple gazing on truth"). This seems to imply that it is an immediate and direct knowledge of truth and consequently infused, but in a broader sense *intuitus* may stand for the knowledge that is obtained without mental discourse and without reasoning, and that is the way we understand it in connection with acquired contemplation.

D. Two Kinds of Acquired Contemplation

168. Contemplation follows either the positive or the negative method. Positive contemplation attributes to God in a supereminent way the perfections perceived in His creature; negative contemplation consists in denying God all limitations and restrictions and comparisons with the perfection of created things. It seems that acquired contemplation commonly follows the negative way, whereas infused contemplation is ordinarily positive.

[9] *Subida del Monte Carmelo,* II, 14, 2.

These two methods of contemplation are, owing to an old and classical distinction, well known to the Neoplatonists and expressed by St. Augustine in these words: "God is ineffable; it is easier to say what He is not than what He is." [10] Dionysius the Pseudo-Areopagite speaks of these two kinds of contemplation in his *Mystical Theology* (chap. 2):

This is truly to see and to know, to praise him who is above nature in a manner above nature, by the abstraction of all that is natural; as those who would make a statue out of natural stone cut off all the surrounding material which hinders the sight of the shape lying concealed within, and by that abstraction alone reveal its hidden beauty. It is necessary, I think, to make this abstraction in a manner precisely opposite to that in which we deal with the divine attributes; for we add them together, beginning with the primary ones, and passing from them to the secondary and so to the last. Here, however, we ascend from the last to the first, abstracting all, so as to unveil and know that which is beyond knowledge and which in all things is hidden from our sight by that which can be known, and so to behold that supernatural darkness which is hidden by all such light as in created things.

The illustration of the statue had been used also by Plotinus [11] even before the time of Pseudo-Dionysius. The author of *The Cloud of Unknowing* advises the attainment of a loving knowledge of God by means of negative contemplation:

Leave thine outward wits and work not with them, neither within nor without: for all those that set them to be ghostly workers within, and ween that they should either hear, smell, see, taste, or feel ghostly things, either within them or without, surely they are deceived and work wrong against the course of nature. . . . Have a man never so much ghostly understanding in knowing of

[10] *Enarrat. in Ps.* 85.
[11] *De pulchritudine,* VII.

all made ghostly things, yet may he never by the work of his under-standing come to the knowing of an unmade ghostly thing: the which is nought but God. But by the failing he may. Because that thing that he faileth in is nothing else but only God. And therefore it was that St. Denis said: "The most godly knowing of God is that which is known by unknowing."

E. WONDERFUL EFFECTS OF CONTEMPLATION

169. Contemplation is the prayer of a perfect soul. Such a soul is like a well-tuned instrument which at the slightest touch renders a perfect tone with overtones and harmonics that linger on and blend softly in a beautiful harmony. A simple word, a single thought, are enough to stir the soul to a profound and devout contemplation, the effects of which are felt for hours and for days.

Meditation wearies and fatigues the mind, and its acts are of short duration; but those of contemplation, even such as is of a common order [acquired contemplation] last whole hours without labor and without weariness; and in the purest souls contempla-tion may easily continue several days together, in the very midst of the world and the engagements of business. In the state of glory, the first act made by a holy soul on beholding the Beatific Vision will last through all eternity without satiety or fatigue, ever the same and ever new. Now contemplation is a participation [by analogy] in the state of glory. It resembles it in its facility and duration. It injures neither health nor strength. . . . Contempla-tion leads souls to heroic acts of charity, zeal, penance, and other virtues, as, for example, martyrdom.[12]

F. SOME PRACTICAL RULES REGARDING ACQUIRED CONTEMPLATION

170. Acquired contemplation is accessible to all. This fact produces a reconciliation between pure asceticism

[12] *The Spiritual Teaching of Father Louis Lallemant,* ed. by Alan G. Mc-Dougall.

and mysticism; it is one of the principal elements of unity and continuity in the two branches of the spiritual science. Alvare de Paz calls it *inchoata contemplatio,* but his description corresponds to what we have said of acquired contemplation: "With regard to the beginning of contemplation, in which a person leaves all reasoning and keeps himself in the presence of our Lord Christ or of the Blessed Trinity, with his heart burning with love, it seems certain to me that a soul purified from its vices, freed from bad and unruly affections, and adorned with virtues, can, and ought, after having practiced meditation, try to attain it." [13]

The expression "incipient contemplation" did not find favor among contemporary authors, but it is interesting because it shows that acquired contemplation is in close relation to infused contemplation even though it is distinct from it. Cardinal Bona calls acquired contemplation *rationativa,* and infused contemplation *experimentalis;* but such expressions are evidently the equivalent of active and passive.[14]

171. Acquired contemplation, being an active form of prayer, is subject to distractions and aridities. These are the common trials of all forms of active prayer and must be borne with patience, humility, and serenity. At the same time one must examine one's conscience to discover their cause. This may be merely a natural one, like fatigue, lack of a remote and proximate preparation, a distracted life. Such natural causes can and ought to be removed.

[13] Vol. III, Bk. V, Part II, chap. 13.
[14] *Haec contemplatio dividitur in acquisitam et infusam. Acquisitam voco quam propria industria et exercitatione, sed non sine divina cooperatione et gratia acquirimus; infusam quae ex sola gratia sive inspiratione divina promanat. . . . Illa rationativa dicitur, ista experimentalis* (*Via comp. ad Deum,* chap. 10, no. 2).

The cause may be preternatural; it may be the devil, who takes advantage of our natural tedium and disgust in order to make us give up prayer and mortification in general, or it may be God Himself who tries our loyalty by such means. Aridity is nothing but spiritual desolation during prayer. Saints and great contemplatives have suffered such trials and often for a long time. The pain of such trials is felt more acutely by those souls that have already enjoyed all the divine consolation and sweetness of prayer. St. Theresa calls them intolerable: "I know . . . that the afflictions God lays on the contemplatives are intolerable; and of such a kind that unless He gave them this repast of sweet spiritual food they could not be endured." [15] These trials are found in every stage of the spiritual life but in different forms and degrees: "They who are in the beginning, the middle, and the end, have their crosses to carry: the crosses however are different." [16]

Distractions are found also in the mystical prayer of quiet, the first kind of infused contemplation. St. Theresa says that she knows no remedy for them.[17] When no specific remedy is found against distractions and aridities, the universal remedy of praying must be employed.

172. For acquired contemplation there is scarcely any need of preludes or special colloquies because, unlike meditation, contemplation is practically never concluded; it lingers on, and life becomes almost a continuous prayer. This is possible because the form of prayer is so simple and transcendent: a loving gaze upon God and divine things. On account of such simplification it has been

---

[15] *Camino de perfeccion*, 18.
[16] St. Theresa, *Vida*, chap. 11.
[17] *Ibid.*, chap. 17.

called also the prayer of simplicity or of simple regard. St. Jane Frances de Chantal seems to be alluding to this prayer when she writes: "I tell you in confidence and in all simplicitly, that it is about twenty years since God took from me all power to accomplish anything in prayer with my mind and with consideration and meditation; and that all I can do is to suffer and to stay my spirit very simply in God, cleaving to this operation by an entire committal, without making acts, unless I should be incited thereto by His motion." [18]

173. The nature of infused contemplation and its various degrees and effects will be explained in mystical theology. Here we must mention what might be termed mixed contemplation. In the course of ordinary acquired contemplation, divine flashes of brief duration in the form of infused contemplation may be experienced occasionally. These are of a mystical nature taken by themselves, but joined with the remaining part of active contemplation they may rightly be called mixed contemplation. This form, however, is a transitory one; it indicates the passage from active to passive contemplation, when such a passage is granted by God.

[18] Letter to a superior, 282; ed. Blaise.

CHAPTER XIII

THE GIFTS OF THE HOLY GHOST

"And the Spirit of the Lord shall rest upon him:
the spirit of wisdom and of understanding,
the spirit of counsel and of fortitude,
the spirit of knowledge and of godliness.
And he shall be filled with the spirit of
the fear of the Lord." [1]

174. This prophecy of Isaias is the classical testimony from Sacred Scripture in proof of the seven gifts of the Holy Ghost. The number seven, like many other numbers in Sacred Scripture, does not mark a limit to the action of the Holy Ghost, which is infinite, but denotes a plenitude. We treat of this subject at this point in our course, not because the action of the Holy Ghost and His gifts are limited exclusively to the unitive way, but because they are more manifest in the perfect soul which has attained the way of union.

The gifts of the Holy Ghost are supernatural habits whereby the soul (intellect and will) is disposed and ready to obey the inspirations of the Holy Spirit, that is, the soul becomes amenable and responds promptly to the motion and the assistance received from the Holy Ghost. These supernatural habits are called gifts because they are not acquired but are infused into the soul together with habitual sanctifying grace and are lost with

[1] Isa. 11:2 f.

it. They are distinct from the infused habits of virtue (theological and moral), explained thus by St. Thomas: "The gifts are distinguished from the virtues by the fact that the virtues contribute to the performance of the act in a human way, but the gifts in a preterhuman way." [2] In his *Summa* the Angelic Doctor states the difference thus: "Virtues are distinguished from the gifts by the fact that the gifts are habits by which man is disposed to follow promptly the inspiration (*instinctum atque motionem*) of the Holy Ghost: the virtues on the other hand are habits by which man is disposed to obey promptly the command and the motion of reason." [3]

Virtues and gifts are infused habits. The term "gift" is used to denote the manner in which these supernatural habits are obtained from God, as a free gift. From this point of view, says St. Thomas in the same article of the *Summa* quoted above, the infused virtues also could be called gifts and there is no distinction between them. The difference, therefore, lies only in the *modus agendi,* which is according to reason for the virtues and according to God for the gifts.

175. It must be admitted, however, that this distinction between virtues and gifts as defended by St. Thomas is only probable. In fact, the Scotists deny any such distinction and, according to Sylvius, their opinion also is to be considered probable. Therefore it cannot be considered wise or scientific to build the entire explanation of mystical theology in general and of infused contemplation in particular on the difference between the virtues and the gifts, a difference which, according to some, is

[2] *III Sent.*, D.34, q.1, a.1.
[3] Ia IIae, q.68, a.1.

improbable, and according to others only probable. This is what Garrigou-Lagrange and the others mentioned in the preceding chapter have tried to do, that is, to explain the whole difference between ascetical and mystical theology, between acquired and infused contemplation, on the basis of the manifestation of the infused virtues in the ascetical life, and of the gifts in the mystical life. Even admitting as probable St. Thomas' opinion on the subject, as we do, some new element in the form of divine illumination and attraction seems to be necessary to explain mystical facts and phenomena.

176. No matter what the opinion of the theologians on this question, the fact remains that the soul's behavior in the unitive way appears more Godlike. In the practice of heroic acts of virtue the soul seems to be guided by the Holy Ghost, whose motion and inspiration it now better understands and more readily obeys. We have already mentioned that in the unitive way the soul is guided by charity, which, as St. Paul says, is given us by the Holy Ghost.[4] The Spirit of charity that kindles the heart of the faithful is also the Spirit of truth that illumines and directs the minds of the saints, and this Spirit dwells within us: "The Spirit of truth, whom the world cannot receive, because it seeth Him not, nor knoweth Him: but you shall know Him; because He shall abide with you, and shall be in you." [5] He is in the soul of each of the faithful who is in the state of habitual grace, but His action is not so manifest when the soul is not yet perfectly mortified and purified, when the senses have not yet been subjected to reason through the practice of virtue. When all this has

[4] Rom. 5:5.
[5] John 14:17.

been done, the reason itself is subjected to God and becomes docile and amenable to the inspiration of the Holy Spirit; it is then that the gifts prevail over the virtues.

177. The theological virtues of faith, hope, and charity are greater than the gifts of the Holy Ghost and to be preferred to them; but the gifts are better than all the other moral virtues.[6]

A. CLASSIFICATION OF THE GIFTS

178. There are four intellective and three volitive gifts, so divided to correspond to the soul's faculties, upon which they act. The four intellective gifts are those of wisdom, understanding, knowledge, and counsel. The three volitive or affective gifts are the gifts of fortitude, godliness, and fear of the Lord. The following is their relation to the theological and cardinal virtues. The gift of wisdom perfects the virtue of charity; the gift of understanding perfects the virtue of faith; the gift of fear perfects the virtue of hope; the gift of counsel perfects the cardinal virtue of prudence; the gift of godliness perfects the virtue of justice (religion); the gift of fortitude perfects the virtue of fortitude; the gift of knowledge perfects the virtue of temperance.[7] Wisdom is the highest and most perfect gift; the least perfect is the gift of fear. The gifts perfect not only the cardinal virtues enumerated above but also all the moral virtues related to them.

The three intellective gifts of wisdom, knowledge, and understanding assist the soul in contemplation. This truth is evident in the case of acquired contemplation. Authors of the opposite school of thought maintain that infused

---

[6] Cf. St. Thomas, *ibid.*, a.8.
[7] Cf. *Summa theol.*, IIa IIae.

contemplation is also produced by these three gifts. It seems more probable, however, that these gifts simply dispose the soul for infused contemplation and that something else is required over and above the action of the gifts, as will be explained in its proper place. All the gifts place the soul under the direct action of the Holy Ghost. The soul being perfect, free from the senses and ready to obey, is well disposed for any motion from above whatever its nature and purpose, including mystical union and infused contemplation. The assistance of the Holy Ghost in prayer in general and in acquired contemplation in particular seems to be indicated in the words of St. Paul: "Likewise the Spirit also helpeth our infirmity. For we know not what we should pray for as we ought; but the Spirit Himself asketh for us with unspeakable groanings. And he that searcheth the hearts knoweth what the Spirit desireth; because He asketh for the saints according to God." [8] This "asking" of the Spirit "according to God" in the souls of His saints is a wordless prayer, a loving gaze, an ardent longing: a kind of prayer of simple regard, or contemplation as explained in the preceding chapter.

179. The gift of wisdom perfects the virtue of charity and is intimately related to it. Since charity is, so to speak, the soul of all supernatural virtues, it follows that the gift of wisdom perfects all other virtues through charity; and as charity is the greatest of all virtues, so is wisdom the greatest of all gifts. Wisdom is a sweet and tasteful science or knowledge of divine and spiritual things. "He who knows the highest cause in a particular genus, and is thereby able to judge and set in order all the things that belong to that genus, is said to be wise in that genus, for

[8] Rom. 8:26 f.

instance, in medicine or architecture. . . . On the other hand, he who knows the cause that is simply the highest, which is God, is said to be wise simply, because he is able to judge and set in order all things according to divine rules." [9]

180. Wisdom is primarily in the intellect as in its subject but it is also in the will by way of effect. This gift of wisdom is so connected with charity that when charity is lost through sin, wisdom is lost also because "wisdom will not enter into a malicious soul, nor dwell in a body subject to sins." [10] To commit a sin is to act like a fool, because folly, according to St. Thomas,[11] is contrary to wisdom and it implies "apathy in the heart and dullness in the senses." [12] That the gift of wisdom perfects all the virtues and, to some extent, contains the other gifts, is manifest from the Book of Wisdom: "It is she [wisdom] that teacheth the knowledge of God, and is the chooser of His works. . . . And if sense do work, who is a more artful worker than she of those things that are? And if a man love justice: her labors have great virtues. For she teacheth temperance and prudence and justice and fortitude, which are such things as men can have nothing more profitable in life." [13] And in the Book of Proverbs the same Wisdom says of herself: "I, wisdom, dwell in counsel, and am present in learned thoughts. The fear of the Lord hateth evil. . . . Counsel and equity is mine, prudence is mine, strength is mine. . . . I love them that love me: and they that in the morning early watch for me shall find me." [14]

[9] *Summa theol.*, IIa IIae, q.45, a.1.
[10] Wisd. 1:4.
[11] *Summa theol.*, IIa IIae, q.46, a.1.
[12] *Ibid.*
[13] Wisd. 8:4–7.
[14] Prov. 8:12–17.

From what has been said, it is clear that the gift of wisdom is far more than the gifts of understanding and knowledge, which are both perfective of faith and purely intellective.

181. The way to cultivate the gifts of the Holy Ghost and particularly the gift of wisdom is both negative and positive. The negative way consists in avoiding everything that may grieve the Holy Spirit, such as deliberate venial sins and attachment to creatures. In this the Holy Spirit is grieved because He sees His action opposed and in danger of being extinguished.

The positive way consists in praying and asking for the gifts of the Holy Ghost, as we do in the *Veni Creator* and in the sequence *Veni, Sancte Spiritus, et emitte coelitus,* in observing recollection both interiorly and exteriorly, looking at all things from a divine point of view. But the most positive way is to practice the moral virtues and to check all manifestations of sensuality, for "the sensual man perceiveth not these things that are of the Spirit of God." [15]

A cheerful and happy disposition of heart and mind in all things that concern God's service and the advancement of our soul is most pleasing to the Holy Spirit, whereas He is grieved by a contrary disposition.

When the doubting man attempts any deed, and fails in it on account of his doubt, grief enters into that man and he grieves the Holy Spirit, and crushes Him out. On the other hand, when anger enters into a man in regard to any matter, and he is embittered, then grief enters into the heart of the man who was irritated, and he is grieved at the deed which he did, and repents that he has wrought a wicked deed. This grief, then, appears to be accompanied by salvation, because the man, after having done a wicked

[15] I Cor. 2:14.

deed, repented. Both actions grieve the Spirit; doubt, because it did not accomplish its object; and anger grieves the Spirit because it did what was wicked. Both these are grievous to the Holy Spirit —doubt and anger. Wherefore remove grief from you, and crush not the Holy Spirit who dwells in you, lest He entreat God against you, and He withdraw from you. For the Spirit of God who has been granted to us to dwell in this body does not endure grief nor straitness. Wherefore put on cheerfulness, which always is agreeable and acceptable to God, and rejoice in it. For every cheerful man does what is good, and minds what is good, and despises injustice; but the man that is grieved always acts wickedly.[16]

The marvelous effects of the gifts of the Holy Ghost in the human soul are beautifully described by St. Basil the Great in his work on the Holy Spirit:

Through Him [the Holy Ghost] our hearts are lifted, the weak are guided by hand, the proficient are made perfect. He illumines those that have been cleansed from all impurity and through His union with them He renders them spiritual. As a shining and transparent body becomes itself extremely brilliant and resplendent when struck by a ray of light reflecting a new splendour, so also the souls that carry the Spirit within themselves and are illumined by the Spirit, become themselves spiritual and reflect their grace on other people also." [17]

B. FRUITS AND BEATITUDES

182. The fruits of the Holy Ghost and the beatitudes are related to the gifts of the Holy Ghost. According to St. Paul (Greek text),[18] the fruit of the Spirit comprises these nine: charity, joy, peace, patience, benignity, goodness, faith, mildness, temperance. According to the Vulgate they are twelve, three others being added, longanimity, modesty, and continency,—temperance being

[16] Hermas, *Pastor*, X Comm., chap. 2.
[17] *De Spiritu Sancto*, IX, 23.
[18] Gal. 5:22 f.

changed to chastity. If we consider these names, we notice that we have theological virtues (charity and faith), a cardinal virtue (temperance), and moral virtues (patience, benignity, mildness, goodness), and in addition some qualities of the mind, such as joy and peace. Even when they have the name of a virtue, the fruits do not denote an operative habit or disposition but a most perfect and delightful act of virtue. St. Thomas defines the fruits of the Holy Ghost as "any virtuous deeds in which one delights." [19] The fruits, therefore, differ from the virtues and from the gifts themselves in the same way as an act differs from the faculty from which it was elicited. The virtue is the branch producing the fruit. The fruits are considered not so much an effect of virtue, which could be more or less pleasant, but the fruit of it, which under the motion of the Holy Ghost has reached its maturity and is sweet and ripe. In the very beginning the practice of virtue imposes sacrifice and mortification and is often disagreeable to our nature. The acquired habit brings facility and joy, and this is a fruit of the Holy Ghost.

183. The beatitudes, according to St. Thomas,[20] are simply perfect and excellent works which by reason of their perfection are assigned to the gifts rather than to virtues. These perfect Christian deeds are called beatitudes because they lead us in a particular way to the attainment of the true and heavenly beatitude or bliss. Like the gifts, they are acts, not habits. The beatitudes are those enumerated by our Lord in His Sermon on the Mount.[21] The number eight in the present case, as the

[19] *Summa theol.*, Ia IIae, q.70, a.2.
[20] *Ibid.*
[21] Matt. 5:3-10.

number of fruits of the Holy Ghost, does not impose a
limit to the beatitudes but is only a symbol and an expression of what they are.

There is a distinction between the gifts and the beatitudes, but, says Sylvius (on this question), this does not
mean the gifts and the beatitudes are two different things,
for the act of virtue that is a beatitude because of its perfection is also a gift because of its sweetness and delight.
For each beatitude the Lord promises a reward, which is
either eternal bliss itself or a foretaste or beginning of
that bliss in the present life. With the beatitudes the Holy
Ghost puts the final touch to the work of sanctification in
our souls. It is as if the dawn of the eternal day were already rising and filling the thirsting soul with the brilliant
splendors of its golden light.

With the beatitudes we come to the end of the road, the
road of perfection, the end of the unitive way. But we
have reached a perfection that is only relative. Therefore
it is a perfection that can admit of some progress, a perfection never absolutely free from all human frailties,
however small and unwilling.

Many souls may at this point, and even long before,
be admitted to mystical prayer and union and begin another sublime phase of spiritual life; some may obtain
only an occasional glimpse of that life; many spend the
rest of their days in acquired contemplation and in the
union which we have described in this part.

184. Ascetical theology guides the soul only as far as
this union. We have reached the highest peak of Christian
perfection, a state of perfect charity, a state of heroic virtue, sanctity itself. From this point the generous soul will
go from virtue to virtue, from splendor to splendor until

the gates of eternal life are opened to it. But no degree of perfection confers impeccability in this life; hence even at this point of perfect charity the fear of God remains, and it should never be dissociated from charity. This is not the servile fear that is excluded by charity [22] when perfect, but the filial fear of children that is the result of perfect love.

[22] I John, 4:18.

CHAPTER XIV

DISCERNMENT OF SPIRITS [1]

185. The doctrine that the Holy Ghost, through inspirations, motions, and various promptings guides the souls of the faithful calls our attention to the fact that many other promptings of a different nature often urge the soul to good or evil. It is important to recognize the nature of the source of such promptings that we may not be misguided. The source is either God, as we have seen, or the devil, or our own nature through its threefold concupiscence. The power to discriminate among these various sources is called discernment of spirits. It may be either infused or acquired. Infused discernment of spirits is one of the charismata mentioned by St. Paul.[2] The acquired power is the result of personal experience.

186. St. John the Apostle [3] warns the faithful against the "spirit of error" and begs them not to believe every spirit: "Dearly beloved, believe not every spirit, but try the spirits if they be of God: because many false prophets are gone out into the world. . . . And every spirit that

---

[1] Dionysius the Carthusian, *De discretione et examinatione spirituum* (Opera, Vol. XL); St. Ignatius, *Spiritual Exercises;* Scaramelli, *Discernimento degli spiriti;* St. Francis de Sales, *Love of God,* Bk. VIII, chaps. 10–14; Saudreau, *Degrees of Spiritual Life,* I, 211 ff.; Tanquerey, *The Spiritual Life,* pp. 951–53, 1281–84; De Guibert, S.J., *Theologia spiritualis ascetica et mystica* (1939), pp. 142–61; *Imitation of Christ,* III, 54. Cf. St. Thomas, *Summa theol.,* Ia IIae, q. 80, a. 4.
[2] I Cor. 12:10.
[3] I John 4:1–6.

dissolveth Jesus, is not of God. . . . He that knoweth
God, heareth us. He that is not of God, heareth us not.
By this we know the spirit of truth and the spirit of error."
The spirit of error of the false prophets is usually the devil,
called Antichrist by St. John. Yet we must not make the
mistake of believing that all promptings to evil come from
the devil directly. Many of them have their origin in our
own nature. The fact is beautifully illustrated by Origen
in his *De principiis:*

Must we suppose that the devil is the cause of our feeling hunger or thirst? Nobody, I think, will venture to maintain that. If,
then, he is not the cause of our feeling hunger and thirst, wherein
lies the difference when each person has reached the age of pu-
berty, and that period has called forth the incentives of natural
heat? It will certainly follow, that as the devil is not the cause of
our feeling hunger and thirst, so neither is he the cause of that
appetite which naturally arises at the time of maturity, namely,
the desire of sexual union. Now it is certain that this cause is not
always so set in motion by the devil that we should be obliged to
suppose that bodies would not possess a desire of that kind if the
devil did not exist. . . . I am of the opinion, indeed, that the same
course of reasoning must be understood to apply to other natural
impulses, as those of covetousness, or of anger, or of sorrow, or of
all those generally which through the vice of intemperance exceed
the natural bounds of moderation. . . . Therefore, as in good
things the human will is of itself weak to accomplish any good (for
it is by divine help that it is brought to perfection in everything),
so also in things of an opposite nature we receive certain initial
elements and, as it were, seeds of sin, from those things which we
use agreeably to nature; but when we have indulged them beyond
what is proper and have not resisted the first movements to intemperance, then the hostile power, seizing the occasion of this first
transgression, incites and presses us hard in every way, seeking to
extend our sins over a wider field.[4]

[4] *De principiis,* III, 2.

187. The prompting of the evil spirit often takes its beginning in natural desires, which may easily lead to intemperance or other transgressions. The devil can be held responsible for all evil suggestions only indirectly, because he offered the occasion for man's first sin, which brought about the fall of our nature. It is like fixing the blame for a fire on the man who has dried the wood that someone else set ablaze.[5] But both the Old and the New Testaments speak of diabolical suggestions: he seduced Eve, he tempted Christ in the desert.

188. Our higher nature (the spirit) and our lower nature (the flesh) are the two principal sources of our interior promptings: "The flesh lusteth against the spirit: and the spirit against the flesh; for these are contrary one to another: so that you do not the things that you would."[6] In the same place St. Paul enumerates the "works of the flesh" toward which its promptings are directed. In opposition to these he puts the "fruits of the Spirit," which are nothing but the fruits of the Holy Ghost explained in the preceding chapter. We see, therefore, how the Spirit of God allies Himself to our spirit and inclines it to "charity, joy, peace, patience, benignity, goodness, longanimity, mildness, faith, modesty, continency, chastity."[7] But the works of the flesh, toward which the lower nature inclines, are "fornication, uncleanness, immodesty, luxury, idolatry, witchcrafts, enmities, contentions, emulations, wraths, quarrels, dissensions, sects, envies, murders, drunkenness, revilings, and such like."[8] Any prompting toward any of these or similar works of the flesh can

[5] St. Thomas, *loc. cit.*
[6] Gal. 5:17.
[7] *Ibid.* (in the Vulgate).
[8] *Ibid.*

come only from our flesh, with which the spirit of evil is often allied. This teaching of St. Paul was beautifully embodied in the *Shepherd of Hermas* in the middle of the second century of our era, under the symbolism of the two angels:

"There are two angels with every man—one of justice and one of iniquity."

And I said to him: "How, sir, am I to know the powers of these, for both angels dwell with me?"

"Hear," said he, "and understand them. The angel of justice is gentle and modest, meek and peaceful. When, therefore, he ascends into your heart, he talks to you of righteousness, purity, chastity, contentment, and of every righteous deed and glorious virtue. When all these ascend into your heart, know that the angel of justice is with you. These are the deeds of the angel of justice. Trust him, then, and his works. Look now at the works of the angel of iniquity. First, he is wrathful and bitter and foolish, and his works are evil, and ruin the servants of God. When, then, he ascends into your heart, know him by his works."

And I said to him: "Sir, I do not know how I shall perceive him."

"Hear and understand," said he. "When anger comes upon you, or harshness, know that he is in you; and you will know this to be the case also when you are attacked by a longing after many transactions and the richest delicacies and drunken revels and divers luxuries and things improper and by a hankering after women and by overreaching and pride and blustering and by whatever is like these. When these ascend into your heart, know that the angel of iniquity is in you." [9]

The same idea occurs again in the form of the twofold desire: "Put away from you all wicked desire, and clothe yourself with good and chaste desire." [10]

[9] Comm. VI, chap. 2.
[10] Comm. XII.

St. Athanasius speaks repeatedly of the necessity of discerning the good from the evil spirit.[11] Cassianus treats of the necessity and nature of the discernment of spirits.[12]

189. The discernment of spirits does not consist in discovering the nature or source of the interior promptings after the deed they suggested has been executed; no special gift is required for such discernment; anyone having a sound judgment can easily discover the cause after seeing the effect.[13] The gift of discernment, acquired or infused, enables the soul to tell whether or not an interior prompting is bad when it first manifests itself, and appears good to others.[14]

190. The "spirits" are inspirations to good deeds or to deeds apparently good but actually evil and an obstacle to good, or to evil itself. Except in the first case, these "spirits" or promptings are nothing but temptations, and they must be dealt with as such.

The discernment of spirits is necessary also in judging various phenomena of the mystical life, such as visions, locutions, revelations, and the origin of the spiritual consolations or desolations experienced sooner or later by every devout soul.

191. The saints, like St. Ignatius Loyola, and authors of the spiritual life, like Scaramelli, have formulated some rules for the discernment of the good and the evil spirits operating in the human soul. Scaramelli has collected

[11] *Vita S. Antonii*, chaps. 22, 35, 37.
[12] *Collationes*, I, 16–23; II (entire).
[13] *Non enim magnum est tunc eum dignoscere, cum ad aliqua pervenerit vel perduxerit, quae sunt contra bonos mores vel regulam fidei; tunc enim a multis discernitur.* St. Augustine, *De Gen. ad litt.*, 12, 13, 28. Bk. XII, chap. 14.
[14] *Illo autem dono, in ipso primordio quo multis adhuc bonus apparet, continuo dijudicatur an malus sit. Ibid.*

from his predecessors the various signs whereby they may
be recognized.[15] We list these signs in parallel columns.

The good spirit	The evil spirit
1. is true;	is false;
2. never prompts useless things;	prompts things that are useless and vain;
3. illumines the mind; leaves the imagination in the dark sometimes.	darkens the mind or gives a false light to the imagination.
4. The mind is amenable.	The judgment is obstinate.
5. Prudence and discernment.	Exaggerations, excesses.
6. Humble thoughts and feelings.	Proud and vain thoughts.

This is the difference between the good and the evil spirits
with regard to the mind. The following are the signs of the
two spirits with regard to the will.

The good spirit	The evil spirit
1. Interior peace.	Perturbation, agitated mind.
2. True, practical humility.	Pride or false humility in words.
3. Confidence in God with diffidence of oneself.	Presumption or despair.
4. An open and docile heart and a flexible will.	An obstinate will; a closed and obdurate heart.
5. A right intention.	A perverse intention.
6. Patience in afflictions.	Impatience.
7. Interior self-denial.	Rebellion of passions.
8. Simplicity and veracity.	Duplicity and simulation.
9. Freedom of the spirit.	The will a slave of worldly affections.
10. Eagerness in imitating Christ.	Alienation from Christ.
11. A meek, benevolent, self-forgetting charity.	A false, bitter, pharisaic zeal.

[15] Scaramelli, *Discernimento degli spiriti,* chaps. 6–9.

192. Experience teaches that a person's virtue and holiness are not always a guaranty against illusions, yet such a person is more recollected and better disposed to hear the voice of God and to discern the good spirit from the evil one. Regarding interior peace and consolations, we find excellent rules of discernment in the *Spiritual Exercises* of St. Ignatius.

Suppose that a soul falls easily into mortal sin, and goes from one fall to another: to plunge it deeper into crime and fill up the measure of iniquity, the infernal enemy ordinarily employs the charms of voluptuousness and all the baits of the senses which he incessantly places before the eyes. On the contrary, to turn him from sin, the good spirit never ceases to prick his conscience with the sting of remorse and the counsels of reason.

But if the soul should decide to make every effort in order to purify itself from its sins, and to advance every day more in the service of God, the evil spirit, to stop and embarrass it, throws in its way every kind of scruple, disquiet, specious pretext, and subject of trouble and agitation. The good spirit, on the other hand, as soon as we begin to amend, encourages, fortifies, consoles, softens even to tears, enlightens the understanding, spreads peace in the heart, smooths all difficulties and obstacles, so that every day more freely, more joyously, and more rapidly, we advance in virtue by the practice of good works.[16]

St. Ignatius gives fourteen rules for the discernment of spirits, applicable to beginners, and eight others for more advanced souls, that is, for that period in spiritual life when the evil spirit often transforms himself into an angel of light to obtain admission in the soul without arousing suspicion: "Aware of the pious desires of the soul, he will begin by seconding them, but soon he will begin to lead it to his own ends." Greater watchfulness and a more rig-

[16] "Rules for the Discernment of Spirits," 2.

orous examination of our thoughts are required at this
time.

With regard to revelations, visions, and locutions, special rules will be given in mystical theology in the chapter
on revelations.

"Put away from you all wicked desires, and clothe yourself with good and chaste desire; for clothed with this desire you will hate wicked desire, and will rein yourself in
even as you wish." [17]

[17] *The Shepherd of Hermas,* Comm. XII.

CHAPTER XV

SCRUPLES; SPIRITUAL DIRECTION

A. SCRUPLES

193. We will get a better understanding of scruples by determining the etymology of the word itself. It is derived from *scrupus* which means a rough stone; *scrupulus,* its diminutive, means a little rough stone, a bit of gravel. Since such small stones are very troublesome in a shoe, the word *scrupulus* signifies difficulty, uneasiness, anxiety. *Scrupulum,* derived from the same word, means the smallest part of a weight or measure.

From this original meaning of the word, we can readily understand how the word *scrupulus* or *scrupulum* came to be employed to denote minute points of behavior or duty. In this sense it implies a good quality or even a great virtue and perfection: "scrupulous" in this sense means to be very exact and conscientious even in smallest matters. This kind of scrupulosity is to be desired and recommended to all who strive after perfection.

194. Scruples are sometimes taken to mean doubts that arise in our mind with regard to the morality or lawfulness of an action. Finally, the term means those promptings of conscience which is led by insufficient motives to discover sin where no sin exists or to regard as a grievous sin what is only a slight venial sin. We treat here of scruples only in this last sense.

195. Scruples indicate an unhealthy condition of the conscience and the practical judgment, which is dangerous and affects the health of body and soul, especially when the victim relies entirely on his own judgment. The only practical remedy is a blind and humble obedience to the advice of his spiritual director. A person who has lost his sight entrusts himself to the guidance of friends who can see; similarly the person whose judgment is clouded by scruples should trust himself to the sound judgment of his director, who is a true spiritual friend. But the difficulty is this, that the blind person is aware of his condition, whereas the scrupulous person is unaware of his state and thinks himself not understood or misjudged; hence he does not easily follow his confessor's or director's advice.

196. Scruples are one of the trials of spiritual life. They may arise either in the beginning of the purgative way or later, when the soul is far advanced in virtue. They constitute one of the passive trials of spiritual purgation not only in ascetical but also in mystical life. If they remain uncured for too long a time, grave disorders in body and soul result. Scruples gradually weaken the nerves and bring on a sense of depression bordering sometimes on despair or insanity. The whole spiritual life is then reduced to finding faults with oneself and visualizing eternal perdition.

197. The causes of scruples are either natural or preternatural. Among the natural causes are physical debility, which may cause nervous prostration and mental depression impairing sound judgment. A contributing cause may be ignorance or confused knowledge of moral principles, a natural inclination to melancholy, hidden pride. The preternatural causes are either God, who thereby wishes to try the soul and purge it, or the devil. If accepted with humility, patience, and submission, scruples leave the soul purified and determined to avoid even the least willful fault. If the devil is the cause of the scruples, his purpose is to hinder the soul's progress and finally to plunge it into discouragement and despair.

198. If the scruples arise from natural causes, then, of course, we must remove the cause so far as we can. If the source is a preternatural one, prayer and humble obedience are the only remedy. The scrupulous person should at least be convinced of that moral principle: *Conscientia dubia, conscientia nulla.* A dubious conscience, as long as the doubt remains, is not a conscience to be followed. A scrupulous person's conscience is never free from doubt; therefore he must blindly obey the spiritual director without arguing.

The scrupulous soul should banish immediately all anxieties and discouragements from the mind and resolve to be always cheerful, kind, and pleasant to everybody, thinking on the beautiful advice of St. Francis de Sales to St. Jane Frances: "You would not offend God for anything in the world; that is quite enough in order to live happily." [1]

St. Alphonsus Liguori, summing up the teaching of saints and theologians, says that an obedient soul has never perished; but disobedience in such critical circumstances may be lead to ruin and despair.[2]

B. SPIRITUAL DIRECTION

199. We mentioned the necessity of spiritual direction when we spoke of the general means of perfection; that

---

[1] Letters, June 24, 1604.
[2] *Praxis confessarii,* no. 95; *Theol. moral.,* II, 16.

was the spiritual direction received by the person desirous
of advancement in virtue. Here we should speak of spiritual direction only in the active sense, as given by the director.

Nobody has expressed more fully and beautifully the
nature and the importance of the difficult art of spiritual
direction than St. Gregory Nazianzen.[3] He begins by saying: "To guide a man seems to me to be the art of arts
and the science of sciences." He proves his assertion by
comparing the care of souls with the care of bodies or
with the duties of the medical profession, showing how
much more difficult and more noble is the former because
of its supernatural end and the very nature of soul and
body. The spiritual director is the physician of souls, not,
however, in the mere natural order; for in that case he
would be more or less of a psychiatrist. He is rather the
physician of souls that are elevated to the supernatural
order and tending to a supernatural goal with supernatural means while still in this world and encumbered with
natural difficulties and obstacles of various kinds.

A good physician must know how to keep the body in
health and how to cure it when it is diseased. He must
know the nature of the various diseases, their symptoms,
their cure. He must know what nourishment is to be ad-
ministered to the sick and the convalescent, to the child,
the adult, and the aged. He must be careful not to yield
to the wishes and desires of the sick, but have the courage
to cut and to burn when such extreme remedies are required to save the patient's life. The physician of souls
must possess a corresponding knowledge and skill with
regard to spiritual health, spiritual diseases, their symp-

[3] *Oratio 2, apologetica*, 16–31.

toms and their remedies. But there is more, because in spiritual life the same disease may require a different treatment according to the sex, age, or social state of the individual, whether he is single or married, a lay person, a religious, or a cleric.

200. No wonder, then, that the number of persons fitted for the office of spiritual director is smaller than may be supposed. The spiritual director's knowledge must comprise all ascetical and mystical theology. This knowledge is ordinarily not acquired by an occasional reading of a spiritual book; it is obtained through systematic study of the subject. He need not have experienced all the ascetical and mystical ways: a physician is not considered a poor physician because he has not suffered the ailment he is trying to cure.

Other qualities of a good spiritual director are prudence, patience, an insight into human nature, boundless charity, firmness of character, and a fixed adherence to supernatural ideas. He must remember that he is an instrument of the Holy Ghost, who is the real director of all souls. Directors are usually persons in holy orders. Ordinary direction is that given in the confessional. The spiritual direction of women, secular or religious, should be limited to the confessional.

A person may choose as spiritual director one who is not his ordinary confessor, but unless the director has a perfect and complete knowledge of the state of conscience and also the past history of a person, his direction cannot be well founded. A general confession or its equivalent made to the spiritual director himself at the beginning will be a great help, otherwise his conclusions and advice may be mistaken.

201. Considering the sublimity and the difficulties of the duties of spiritual director, it is rash for anyone to assume them without the necessary preparation and the required qualities of mind and character. We may repeat today what St. Nilus wrote fifteen centuries ago: "Every kind of art requires time and extensive training in order to be right; only the art of arts is practiced without previous apprenticeship." [4] For St. Nilus, as for St. Gregory Nazianzen, the art of arts is the direction of souls, a thing, he says, which the Apostle St. Paul himself affirms not to have yet understood, while the people of his day claimed to know it quite well because they were unaware of the extent of their own ignorance. This was the reason why spiritual life began to be despised, and anyone who devoted himself to it was ridiculed. (*Ibid.*)

202. A director endowed with the necessary knowledge and prudence will have his own personal method of diagnosing spiritual ailments and judging the state of a person's spiritual health.

When charity is weak, spiritual vitality is weak also. It is a sign of spiritual malnutrition—some negligence in spiritual duties—or of the presence of venial sins and venial disorderly affections. From the degree of charity one may conclude the degree of perfection in general.

Another important criterion is the state of mental prayer. We have seen in the preceding chapters how each of the three ways has its own form of mental prayer. Meditation is the proper prayer of the beginners (purgative way); affective prayer is proper to the proficient (illuminative way); acquired contemplation is the prayer of perfect souls (unitive way). Any form of passive, infused

---

[4] St. Nilus, *De monastica exercitatione*, chap. 22.

contemplation is a sign of the mystic state and mystic union.

203. Evidently those in the unitive way and the beginners in the purgative way should not receive the same direction, just as the food of the adult cannot be the same as the food of an infant. Nor can the mystics be guided according to the same rules as others in every respect. Once the spiritual director has learned the duties and the difficulties of the various stages of the spiritual life and also the personal difficulties and graces of the individual soul seeking his guidance, it should not be difficult to direct it. The golden rule of direction is: Firmness with kindness, or *fortiter in re, suaviter in modo.*

We may add here the words of that most lovable saint, who in his days directed countless souls and many of them to great sanctity, St. Philip Neri.

> I do not like confessors to make the ways of virtue too difficult, especially to those who are newly converted. They should not irritate them with anything like harshness. . . . Let us, on the contrary, use our every effort to gain them to Christ by compassion and sympathy, by sweetness and love; let us stoop down to them as far as we can; let our aim be to enkindle in their hearts the love of God, which alone can enable them to do great things.[5]

St. Francis de Sales sums up the requisites of a good spiritual director by saying: "He must be full of charity, of knowledge, and of prudence; if one of these three qualities be wanting in him, there is danger." [6]

St. Theresa requires that her spiritual directors should possess knowledge above everything else. She was mindful of her own painful experience with ignorant and inex-

---

[5] Capecelatro, *Life of St. Philip Neri,* I, 363.
[6] *Devout Life,* Part I, chap. 4.

perienced confessors especially with regard to mystical knowledge. Hence, even while exhorting her spiritual daughters to seek direction, she insists on this quality: "Endeavor to treat on the affairs of your soul with a confessor who is spiritual and learned." [7]

[7] *Avisos,* 63.

PART III

AMPLIFICATION OF SEVERAL QUESTIONS FOR ADDITIONAL READING

CHAPTER XVI

THE MEANING OF ASCETICISM

204. A short and clear definition of words with a long history, full of vicissitudes, has always been difficult. This is precisely the case with the word "asceticism." The Greek verb *askein*, from which asceticism finally derives, was in common use in the days of Homer. Greek philosophers, as we pointed out in the beginning of this book, made an extensive use of it, paving the way for the full meaning it later acquired in Christian literature.

205. The Stoic philosopher Epictetus, who lived in Rome at the time of Nero, has a special chapter on Ascetic Exercise in his work entitled *Moral Discourses*.[1] He warns his disciples not to carry their exercise beyond nature, or merely to attract admiration. What was the nature of these ascetic exercises? Here are some of the examples he gives. Am I inclined to pleasure? I will bend myself beyond a due proportion to the other side for the sake of exercise. Am I averse to pain? I will break and exercise those appearances that strike my mind so as to overcome my aversion. Who is an ascetic, according to Epictetus? He who endeavors to restrain desire completely, and to apply aversion only to things dependent on choice. He observes with great wisdom that different persons are to be exercised in different ways. These exercises are the

[1] The teaching of Epictetus was compiled and published by Arrian, one of his disciples.

askesis, the Stoic asceticism. On the whole, it is a well proportioned and beautiful body, but without a soul.

206. At the very beginning of the Christian era, Philo, the Jewish philosopher, insists not only on the philosophical but also on the religious element of asceticism. He considers asceticism a methodical effort, along the lines of moral and religious faith, which, while perfecting the human soul, prepares it for the contemplation of God and mystical elevation. The ascetical mind is that which frees itself progressively from the world of the senses. For Philo, as for Seneca, the ascetic is a person who has already made some moral progress; he belongs to an intermediate category between the bad and the perfect.

207. Epictetus, Philo, and Seneca were contemporaries of St. Paul. Pagan asceticism, like pagan philosophy, was then making a supreme effort to save itself from destruction, while the world was beginning to awake in the light of the Gospel of Christ.

The verb *askein* does not occur more than once in all the sacred books of the New Testament. In that single instance, the word receives its full Christian meaning, and we obtain the first clear definition of Christian asceticism.[2] It was St. Paul who gave us this definition. Later, in his Epistles, he developed the idea of Christian asceticism by his several allusions to the athleticism of his day, to convey the idea of spiritual endeavor: "Know you not that they that run in the race, all run indeed, but one receiveth the prize? So run that you may obtain. And every one that striveth for the mastery, refraineth himself from all things: and they indeed that they may receive a corruptible crown; but we an incorruptible one. I there-

[2] Acts 24:16.

fore so run, not as at an uncertainty: I so fight, not as one
beating the air. But I chastise my body, and bring it into
subjection: lest perhaps, when I have preached to others,
I myself should become a castaway." [3] The efforts, sacri-
fices, and renunciations of the athletes of the stadium and
palestra of old are set as an example to Christian endeavor
in winning an incorruptible crown. Lest perhaps any
doubt should remain as to the meaning of the Christian
athleticism, he explains its first essential element, which
is self-denial and mortification, the subjection of the flesh
with its inordinate desires. A similar allusion is found in
his Epistle to the Philippians. [4] That such were not merely
the sentiments of his younger days but of his whole life,
is manifest from what he wrote to his disciple Timothy
from Rome, during his second imprisonment, near the end
of his life: "I am even now ready to be sacrificed: and
the time of my dissolution is at hand. I have fought a good
fight, I have finished my course, I have kept the faith." [5]

208. It is not surprising, therefore, that St. Clement
of Rome finds no better word to designate the great heroes
of the Neronian persecution than the word athlete. [6] The
great martyr Ignatius, in writing to Polycarp, another
candidate for martyrdom, uses the same expression: "Be
thou watchful as an athlete of God." [7]

With Clement of Alexandria and Origen the word
askesis takes on the precise and current Christian meaning. In the strict sense of the word, asceticism, for them,
is a life of continence, of virginity; in a broad sense it

[3] I Cor. 9:24–27.
[4] Phil. 3:13 f.
[5] II Tim. 4:6 f.
[6] *Epistle* (I) *to the Corinthians*, V, 1.
[7] St. Ignatius, *Ad Polycarpum*, II, 2.

means generally a life of fervent piety lived even in the midst of the world.

209. We are now in a position to understand better the meaning of Christian asceticism in the light of the Scriptures of the New Testament. Our asceticism is based principally on the words of our Lord, reported unanimously by the Synoptics: "If any man will follow Me, let him deny himself, and take up his cross, and follow Me." [8] Luke and Mark, who wrote after Matthew, are careful in noting that these words were directed not only to the disciples but to all: "Calling the multitude together with His disciples, He said to them." And He said to all."

Christian asceticism consists of a negative and a positive element. The negative element is self-denial. The positive element is the following of Christ: "Take up his cross, and follow Me." The negative element of asceticism is the subject of frequent exhortations in the writings of the apostles, notably of St. Paul: "To put off, according to former conversation, the old man, who is corrupted according to the desire of error." [9] "But now put you also all away: anger, indignation, malice, blasphemy, filthy speech out of your mouth. Lie not one to another: stripping yourselves of the old man with his deeds." [10]

210. The imitation of Christ remains the supreme aspiration of asceticism, its positive element, and the great motive for self-denial and renunciation. "I beseech you," writes St. Paul to the Corinthians, "be ye followers of me, as I also am of Christ." [11]

[8] Mark 8:34; Matt. 16:24; Luke 9:23. Luke adds the word "daily"; "And he said to all: If any man will come after Me, let him deny himself, and take up his cross daily, and follow Me."
[9] Eph. 4:22.
[10] Col. 3:8 f.
[11] I Cor. 4:16.

St. Peter must have experienced a great satisfaction the day he could tell his Master that both he and his fellow apostles had fulfilled the requirements for Christian asceticism and Christian perfection, the renunciation of all things and the following of Christ: "Behold we have left all things and have followed Thee." [12]

The imitation of Christ is not only a necessary element of asceticism, it is also its most powerful motive. Christ's example is the dynamic or motor idea that moves the soul to embrace with joy and rapture privations, sufferings, all crosses, and death itself. The symbol of the Christian religion is the cross, which is also a symbol of suffering and death. Suffering is an important element of Christian asceticism; without it, asceticism is rightly considered adulterated and false. Suffering, however, does not mean joylessness: "Blessed are they that suffer"; [13] "If also you suffer anything for justice' sake, blessed are ye." [14]

The frequent exhortations of the Gospel to avoid sin and to practice virtue show that the Christian religion is a religion of moral efforts and endeavors, an ascetical religion.

211. Asceticism has its origin in the desire and determination to follow the divine Master and to carry the cross with Him.

From the idea of suffering and carrying the cross grew that of martyrdom, of giving one's life for Christ, of following Him even in death. Martyrdom was the crown of a life of privations and sufferings, the crown of Christian asceticism, and asceticism was the best preparation for

[12] Matt. 19:27.
[13] Matt. 5:10.
[14] I Pet. 3:14.

a martyr's death. Not every Christian, however, could gain the crown of martyrdom. Virginity was soon regarded as its equivalent and was readily adopted by the infant Church as the most exalted ascetical practice. Virginity, as absolute continence, is a lifelong sacrifice, a kind of martyrdom. In the second century we meet Origen describing the life of Christian ascetics as consisting eminently in the profession of virginity or continence: "I will describe," he says, "the mode of life of our ascetics. We often meet with Christians who might marry and thus spare themselves the aggravation of the struggle between the flesh and the spirit. They prefer to refrain from exercising their right, and to lay upon themselves hard penances, to subdue their bodies by fasting, to bring them under obedience by abstinence from certain foods, and thus in every way to mortify by the spirit the works of the flesh." [15]

The practice of continence and virginity was freely adopted by a large number of Christians of both sexes. These people remained in their families in the world and shared the common life of the Christian society. Toward the end of the third century such persons began to withdraw from the world into the desert or to live in an organized community of their own. Virginity was the one great renunciation of Christian asceticism; many other renunciations were demanded by virginity itself that it might remain inviolate to the end. Virgins were the pride and glory of Christian communities. The Fathers of the Church are tireless in the praise of virginity. We learn from St. Justin that continents and virgins were found in all classes of society: "Many men and women from sixty

[15] Origen, *In Jeremiam Proph., Homil.,* XIX, 7.

to seventy years of age, brought up from childhood in the law of Christ, have kept themselves pure. I can show them in all classes of society." [16]

212. In subsequent centuries Christian asceticism has remained essentially the same, regardless of minor accidental changes in exterior form and practices. Monachism and more modern religious congregations and societies of both sexes are schools of Christian asceticism, where both the essence and the exterior form of earlier asceticism are closely imitated. The essence of asceticism for seculars and religious people has been and remains always the same: "to mortify by the spirit the works of the flesh," and to follow Christ.

213. The Protestant principle that faith alone justifies without good works, has dealt the greatest blow to Christian asceticism, the very foundations of which were shaken when the necessity of good works was denied. Not only were such things as celibacy, fasting, and mortifications ridiculed by Protestants, but every moral effort, which is a form of asceticism in the widest sense of the word, was radically discouraged. For this reason the German historian O. Zoeckler, in his work *Askese und Moenchtum,* calls Protestantism a kind of antiasceticism.

In spite of some pietistic currents in several Protestant sects in the last two or three centuries, the great body of Anglo-Saxon Protestantism remains to this day generally averse and even hostile to asceticism.

214. If a good Catholic of our own day were asked to give an account of his moral conduct, he might well use the often quoted words of St. Paul: "I do endeavor to

[16] St. Justin Martyr, *I Apologia,* XV, 6.

have always a conscience without offence towards God and towards men." [17] The synthesis of that constant endeavor was Christian asceticism in the time of the apostles; none other is our Catholic asceticism today.

[17] Acts 24:16.

CHAPTER XVII

THE LOVE OF GOD IN SPIRITUAL LIFE

215. The love of God occupies a central and eminent position in spiritual life. Spiritual life is taken here in both its ascetical and its mystical aspects. On the point of charity, or love of God, asceticism and mysticism do not differ. Love is the bridge linking together the two heights of spiritual endeavor. It is true that a mystic, more than the ordinary ascetic, is guided by love rather than by reasoning, but, *ceteris paribus,* he has no higher degree of divine love than the ascetic who possesses the same amount of divine grace. The difference, if any at all, is not a specific one, nor is it one of degree, but only of manner.

216. Renunciation, the daily cross, the imitation of Christ, these are the substance of asceticism. The love of God is its perfection, its very soul. Before speaking of the love of man for God, we must mention the love of God for man: "Because God first hath loved us." [1] In this respect the position of divine love is as central and supereminent as God Himself, because "God is charity." [2] The love of God for man is made manifest in all of God's works *ad extra.* Reading through the articles of the Apostles' Creed, we have a synthesis of that immortal and glorious history of the love of God for us. That love shines forth

[1] I John, 4:19.
[2] *Ibid.,* 4:16.

in the work of creation, Incarnation, redemption, in the Church, in the communion of saints, in the resurrection of the body, in life everlasting. With the logic of love, the apostle of love rightly concludes, saying: "Let us therefore love God, because God first hath loved us." [3]

217. There is a natural and a supernatural love of God, or love of man for God. The natural love of God is born of the natural knowledge of God as our Creator and benefactor. Michael du Bay, who denied the existence of a natural love of God, was condemned by St. Pius V in 1567, for this and many other false doctrines.[4] Our human reason declares the existence of God; therefore we know naturally that we ought to love Him above all things. The duty of loving God is not limited to Christians, it extends also to indfidels, according to St. Bernard.[5] St. Paul holds the infidels inexcusable, "because that, when they knew God, they have not glorified Him as God, or given thanks." [6] The greatest glorification God expects from His creatures is being loved by them. We have noble examples of pagans who have recognized their obligation of loving God and have probably fulfilled it according to their natural capacity. "Since the soul," says Plotinus, the pagan Neoplatonist, "is different from God and yet derived from Him, it necessarily loves Him. The love which it possesses here is common and vulgar, but in the spiritual life it is filled with celestial love. . . . Alone to the Alone." [7] With no less eloquence and enthusiasm, love and gratitude for God's benefits are acknowledged by Epictetus:

[3] *Ibid.*
[4] Denz., 1034, 1036.
[5] *"Meretur ergo amari propter seipsum Deus, et ab infideli; qui etsi nesciat Christum, scit tamen seipsum." De diligendo Deo,* II, 6.
[6] Rom. 1:21.
[7] VI *Ennead.*

"What words can proportionally express our applauses and praises? For, if we had any understanding, ought we not, both in public and in private, incessantly to sing hymns, and speak well of the Deity, and rehearse His benefits? . . . Since I am a reasonable creature, it is my duty to praise God. This is my business. I do it. Nor will I ever desert this post as long as it is vouchsafed me; and I exhort you to join in the same song." [8] This was the language of love of God in the mouth of a pagan. It does not seem probable that his praises are mere lip-service; they seem to come from the heart and to be a natural expression of love of God. This was human nature left to itself, deprived of the assistance of divine grace and of the supernatural love of God that we call charity. Even in fallen nature, the love of God occupies a central and eminent position.

218. It is particularly of the supernatural love of God, or of charity, that we speak in ascetical theology when we assert that the love of God is the very substance of Christian perfection.[9] Charity is an infused theological virtue which enables us to love God above all things for His own sake, and to love for God's sake ourselves and our neighbor like ourselves. From this definition we learn the prominent and central position of the love of God in the life of a Christian. Charity is like the sun. It extends its light and warmth in all directions. As at daybreak, at the approach of the sun, darkness and shadows go, so at the infusion of charity in the human soul, the shadows of sin and darkness of death disappear. The light and heat

[8] *Moral Discourses,* I, 16, 3.
[9] It is understood that Christian perfection consists in perfect charity. One cannot speak of perfection where charity is still imperfect.

of the sun fill the air in which we live, the sky above, and everything on earth. Charity also has light and warmth of a spiritual and supernatural order, a light and warmth that come from God and are reflected, as from a pure mirror, back to God and to all those whom He has raised to His friendship or to whom He offers it, His saints in heaven, the poor souls in purgatory, here on earth ourselves and all our fellow men whether friends or enemies. It is true that, in the natural order, knowledge, not love, is the source of light for the human soul; but love has a light of its own, and this is particularly true of the love of God. "For when we begin to love the heavenly things we have heard, we know already what we love, because love itself is a kind of knowledge." [10]

219. No Christian perfection is possible without the love of God. However, charity is not the only possible motive of good actions, because charity does not exclude the fear of God or the hope of reward; and any action motivated either by fear or by hope is a good action, though not a perfect ne. Paschasius Quesnel, who held that "without the love of God no good work is possible," was condemned by Clement XI in 1713.[11] Even when the motive is an imperfect one, as in the case of fear and hope, charity is not entirely excluded. It is not a perfect charity but an incipient, an imperfect one, not quite explicit but implicit in fear and hope.

220. Asceticism and the perfection of the love of God are based on the fact that, whereas the *habitus* of charity is infused in the soul by God, the act of charity itself must

---

[10] Dum enim audita supercoelestia amamus, amata iam novimus, quia amor ipse notitia est. St. Gregory the Great, *In Ezech.* II, *Hom.* 27, 4.
[11] Denz., 1394-99.

be produced by man with the assistance of actual grace. It would be Quietism to affirm that the act of faith or charity is produced exclusively by God, and that man must remain in a receptive passivity while striving after perfection. As love, according to St. Augustine and St. Gregory the Great,[12] is the motive power of the soul, the *machina mentis*, setting everything in motion and leading to the most glorious achievements, so is the love of God in spiritual life. By charity, the soul loves God in a supernatural way and thereby communicates with the source of its life. Charity is never in the soul without divine grace. Thus charity is the most beautiful expression of supernatural life, since it is the friendship of man for God.[13] Asceticism and spiritual perfection are recognized as genuine by abiding charity, and their progress is measured by charity. In charity, the law finds its fulfillment: "Love is the fulfilling of the law"; [14] virtue finds its proper form,[15] Christianity its noblest expression, the human heart its activity and repose.

221. Love of God, like love in general, tends toward union. Love is the strongest bond of moral union. The unity of the Church is based not only on the unity of faith and discipline but also on that of charity. It is the love of God that makes all Christians of one heart and one soul.[16] It is charity that breaks down all barriers of social differences, uniting all men under the title of brethren, the only title of nobility known to the early Christians.[17]

---

[12] Machina quippe mentis est vis amoris, quae hanc dum a mundo extrahit, in alta sustollit. St. Gregory the Great, *Moral.*, VI, 37, 58.

[13] St. Thomas, *Summa theol.*, IIa IIae, q.23, a.1.

[14] Rom. 13:10.

[15] St. Thomas, *ibid.*, a.8.

[16] Acts 4:3.

[17] Tertullian, *Apol.*, 39.

222. Because the love of God is something divine, it reaches everywhere. It cannot, like love of self, be limited to the narrow confines of one's breast. In imitation of the Supreme Good, which is supremely *diffusivum sui*, the love of God is diffusive and active by nature. It covers and embraces the world, as the heroic charity of so many saints has shown in every age. It goes to the worlds beyond. Suffering souls are aided by the charity of their living and loving brethren here on earth. Blessed souls in heaven extend their charity to both the militant and the suffering Church in the form of prayer and intercession. The communion of saints is possible because of the charity of the saints. It is love that brings about union of hearts, harmony of spirits, communion of goods. It is the love of God that binds together heaven and earth.

223. "Love itself," says St. Augustine, "can never be idle. What is there in any man good or evil of which love is not the author? I wish you would show me a kind of love that remains idle and doing nothing. . . . Have you perhaps been told: Do not love at all? God forbid. You will be lazy, dead, detestable, miserable if you do not love anything. Love, therefore, but consider well what you love." [18] The love of God has no worse enemy than love itself, when love has turned away from God and is bent upon self or any other creature without any reference to the Creator and with exclusion of Him. It is love turned loose and bent upon destruction of the noblest and most precious thing in man, the friendship of God. This is sin. Sin of whatever form is a denial of divine love. What else is the meaning of that definition: *Aversio a Deo, conversio ad creaturas?* Turning away from a friend and tak-

[18] *Enarrat. in Ps.* 31, 2.

ing someone else in his place: what is this but a breaking of all ties of friendship? Sin, mortal sin, is incompatible with the love of God. As the love of God is spiritual life to the soul, so is sin its spiritual death. But love itself, in one form or another, is eternal, changeable but not destructible. Turned away from God and eternal life, love no longer busies itself with works of life, the works of charity, but with mortal things, with works of death: "Is not love the author of shameful deeds, adulteries, crimes, murders, lustful actions of all kinds?" [19]

224. The love of God is not possible without the love of our neighbor, without the love of man in the widest and limitless sense of the word: "If any man say: I love God, and hateth his brother; he is a liar. For he that loveth not his brother whom he seeth, how can he love God whom he seeth not? And this commandment we have from God, that he who loveth God, love also his brother." [20] These words of the apostle of love are too plain to need any explanation. The actual Christian love of our neighbor proves that our love of God is real and not imaginary, that we are not deceiving ourselves with mere feelings and sentimentalities. If our heart remains closed to one man, it remains closed to God. Since we spend all our life on earth among men, and every day in many ways we must deal with them, it follows that charity must be the Christian rule of our conduct. We cannot sin against our neighbor without sinning against God. The commandment of love is one, only the object is manifold. The act whereby we love God is specifically the same as the act whereby we love our neighbor, because we love him for God's sake,

[19] *Ibid.*
[20] I John 4:20 f.

that he may be in God.[21] There is often something or
other in our neighbor that is not lovable or honorable,
much that is reprehensible and condemnable. All that,
and even more, does not exempt us from loving him, because we do not love him under any such aspect, but the
aspect under which we love him is God. Under this aspect,
everybody is lovable, at all times, under all circumstances.
Under the same aspect, we must love ourselves, and such
love is always ordinate and sacred, always permissible,
always commanded, always possible, even when we discover that we are most unworthy. The love of ourselves
precedes the love of our neighbor and should serve as a
norm and guide in the practice of charity toward our
fellow men. The love of ourselves is the supernatural kind
of love, or charity, not the innate love of self, based on the
natural instinct of self-preservation. This natural love, or
self-love, is often an obstacle to the love of God; in fact,
it is its worst enemy when not restrained and governed
by reason and faith.[22] With a supernatural love, we are
permitted, even commanded, to love ourselves for God's
sake. We must love our immortal souls, created to the
image and likeness of God, redeemed by the Word incarnate, sanctified by the Spirit of God, and destined for
a blessed eternity. Does charity extend to our body? We
answer with St. Thomas: "Our body can be considered
in two ways: first, in respect of its nature, secondly, in

[21] St. Thomas, *Summa theol.*, IIa IIae, q.25, a.1.
[22] *Fecerunt itaque civitates duas amores duo: terrenam scilicet amor sui
usque ad contemptum Dei, caelestem vero amor Dei usque ad contemptum
sui.* St. Augustine. *De Civitate Dei*, XIV, 28.
"The excessive love of self is in reality the source to each man of all offenses;
for the lover is blinded about the beloved, so that he judges wrongly of the
just, the good, and the honorable." Plato, *The Laws*, 5.

respect of the corruption of sin and its punishment. Now the nature of our body was created, not by an evil principle, as the Manichaeans pretend, but by God. Hence we can use it for God's service. . . . Consequently, out of the love of charity with which we love God, we ought to love our body also; but we ought not to love the evil effects of sin and the corruption of punishment; we ought rather, by the desire of charity, to long for the removal of such things." [23]

225. The object of charity is thus defined by St. Augustine: "There are four things to be loved; one which is above us, namely, God, another which is ourselves, a third which is nigh to us, namely, our neighbor, and a fourth which is beneath us, namely, our own body." [24] Charity, no matter what its object, is always a love of God, because we either love God for His own sake or we love our neighbor or ourselves for God's sake. The love of God is the fundamental law of the kingdom of God. It obliges all without exception, subjects as well as superiors. Authority of any nature or rank does not dispense anyone from the law of charity. The administration of justice, the enforcement of the laws, the punishment of transgressors, should never be divorced from charity, which is the form of all virtues. God is love, and love is His law. The Christian religion is based on the love of God and man. Any work performed in the name of Christian religion will pass as such not only because of the marks of the true faith but also because of the marks of charity. Charity proves not only that faith is authentic, but alive: "Charity

---

[23] *Summa theol., loc. cit.*, a.5.
[24] *De doctrina Christiana*, I, 23.

never falleth away: whether prophecies shall be made void or tongues shall cease or knowledge shall be destroyed." [25]

226. Charity is supranational, supraracial, is universal, is in some sense infinite, because it knows no bounds. It is the only virtue that cannot fall into excesses. The due measure of the love of God is to love God without measure.[26] Charity is the central force of Christianity, the central, connective force of all virtuous endeavors for Christian perfection.

[25] I Cor. 13:8.
[26] St. Bernard, *De diligendo Deo*, I, 1. *Vultis ergo a me audire, quare et quomodo diligendus sit Deus? Et ego: causa diligendi Deum, Deus est; modus, sine modo diligere.*

CHAPTER XVIII

THE UNIVERSALITY OF THE OBLIGATION
OF TENDING TO PERFECTION

227. The name Christian, in the most absolute sense of the word, is equivalent to the term saint. According to St. Paul's terminology, a Christian is a saint. In this sense he uses the word "saint" in writing to the many Christian communities of his day: "To all that are at Rome, the beloved of God, called to be saints." [1] "To the Church of God that is at Corinth, to them that are sanctified in Christ Jesus, called to be saints." [2] "To the Church of God that is at Corinth, with all the saints that are in all Achaia." [3] "To all the saints who are at Ephesus." [4] Others books of the New Testament use the word "saint" to designate Christ's disciples in general. A saint is, therefore, in the language of Sacred Scripture, often equivalent to "faithful."

228. The word "saint" implies holiness by dedication, consecration, election, moral sanctity through union with God in perfect charity. Holiness means "wholeness," or completeness, perfection, a goal that every disciple of Christ must strive to reach. In the course of time, saints were called only the perfect Christians, those that had

---

[1] Rom. 1:7 κλητοῖς ἁγίοις, *vocatis sanctis.*
[2] I Cor. 1:2.
[3] II Cor. 1:1.
[4] Eph. 1:1.

lived up to their vocation, and those whose heroic virtues
and holiness of life had been officially and solemnly recognized and approved by the Church. According to St.
Paul, a Christian is one who has been called and dedicated
to sanctity and perfection: *vocatus sanctus*. The term
"saint" is not reserved for the ministers of the Church;
these are mentioned separately from their flock, the common faithful, the saints: "To all the saints in Christ Jesus
who are at Philippi, with the bishops and deacons." [5]
Sacred orders confer a special consecration and sanctity
on the ministers of the Church. Their office imposes upon
them a special obligation of tending to perfection. Every
Christian, however, without distinction of sex, of age, of
social rank, of profession, of temperament, is called to
be a saint, is obliged to strive after Christian perfection.

229. St. Paul exhorts all Christians to sanctity and perfection, reminding them that this is their vocation, this is
the will of God. The will of God, once made manifest,
imposes a sacred duty and obligation upon man. Knowing man's weakness and the infirmity of fallen human
nature, the great Apostle accompanies his exhortations
with prayer and supplications to God: "Therefore we
also . . . cease not to pray for you and to beg that you
may be filled with the knowledge of His will, in all wisdom
and spiritual understanding: that you may walk worthy
of God, in all things pleasing; being fruitful in every good
work and increasing in the knowledge of God. . . . We
preach, admonishing every man and teaching every man
in all wisdom, that we may present every man perfect in
Christ Jesus." [6]

[5] Phil. 1:1.
[6] Col. 1:9 f., 28.

230. These words of St. Paul prove our assertion. He had received a mission from God: "The Church, whereof I am made a minister according to the dispensation of God, which is given to me towards you." [7] His mission was to teach every man in all wisdom, that he may present every man perfect in Christ Jesus. Perfection consists in charity and the imitation of God: "Be ye therefore followers of God as most dear children; and walk in love, as Christ also hath loved us." [8]

231. A Christian is a new man created according to God in justice and truth: "Be renewed in the spirit of your mind: and put on the new man, who according to God is created in justice and holiness of truth." [9] The original justice, lost through sin but restored by Christ, must be made manifest in Christian life. Exhortation to Christian perfection is the most common subject in the epistles of St. Paul and other apostles. Such exhortations presuppose a universal duty on the side of the Christians, the duty of tending to perfection.

232. Should there be any doubt regarding the universality of such obligations among Christians, a summary reading of the *Album sanctorum,*[10] or list of the saints, should be sufficient to dispel all doubts. Among the canonized saints of the Church, we find not only popes, bishops, priests, monks, and nuns, but also kings and emperors, queens and royal princesses, soldiers, lawyers, teachers, artizans, domestic servants, housemaids, merchants, beggars, farmers, physicians, artists, univer-

[7] Col. 1:25.
[8] Eph. 5:1 f.
[9] Eph. 4:23 f.
[10] A relatively complete list of known saints is the *Roman Martyrology.* The most complete list is in *A Biographical Dictionary of the Saints* by F. G. Holweck.

sity professors, married men and women as well as virgins and widows, converted public sinners, innocent boys and girls. These are the facts at the distance of nineteen centuries. Every fact implies its own possibility: *Ab esse ad posse valet illatio.* Christians from every walk of life actually attained to Christian perfection because the road to perfection was open to them all alike. God gave them the necessary graces because it was according to His will that they should tend to perfection.

233. Christian perfection consists in perfect charity, in the perfect love of God and our neighbor. The commandment of love is universal, none is excluded, consequently the obligation of tending to perfection is universal, it affects all Christians. All men must tend to perfection because all men must love God.

234. A man is perfectly free in embracing the Christian religion;[11] but once his choice has been made and he has been baptized, he is bound to live as a Christian, as another Christ, he must tend to perfection according to his vocation and state in life. There is one road for all Christians, that of the cross, one supreme duty, that of following Christ and imitating Him. Tending to perfection means striving to become Christlike, Godlike, perfect in charity. In these general terms, the obligation affects all Christians alike. The commandments of God must be observed by all under pain of losing God's friendship, charity. Now, the perfection of charity, as it has been shown earlier in this volume, consists primarily in the keeping of the commandments. Therefore the obliga-

[11] We speak of freedom in an absolute and physical sense. In this sense, one is free to choose between true and false religion; but in a moral sense, one is bound to accept the true religion once it has been proved such to him.

tion of tending to perfection is universal and not limited
to one class of people.

Christian perfection consists secondarily and instrumentally in observing the evangelical counsels. Every
Christian must have at least the spirit of the counsels in
tending to perfection and actually keep the one or the
other that is compatible with his state in life. The keeping
of all the counsels is the ideal, but they do not oblige all
because they are only counsels. Precepts are for all, counsels for the few.

235. We find this doctrine of the universality of the obligation of tending to perfection not particularly stressed
from the time of the Fathers to our own. We find traces
of the doctrine in St. Thomas, but not an explicit and
extensive treatment of the subject. He says that "the perfection of Christian life consists in charity," and "it is
evident that perfection consists essentially in the observance of the commandments," and that "some have the
perfection of life, who nevertheless have not the state of
perfection." [12] The inference from such principles is evident, but the Angelic Doctor and other Scholastics seem
to be rather reluctant in expressing it. Perhaps the vast
number of Christians who for centuries gave no thought
to the work of perfection, the many Christians spending
their life in sin, may have created the popular impression
that Christian perfection was not meant for all, but only
for those who retire into a convent or monastery to live
under a rule and observe the counsels. Such impression
has not completely disappeared from the mind of the
ordinary Christian even today, and we should do nothing
to encourage it. On the contrary, we consider it a duty

[12] St. Thomas, *Summa theol.,* IIa IIae, q.184, a.2, 3, 4.

to correct that false notion and destroy the "inferiority complex," with regard to Christian perfection, from the mind of the common faithful.

236. The French school of spirituality of the seventeenth century,[13] which has had such a great influence on the spirituality of our own generation, tried to prove our thesis by affirming that a real Christian must be another Christ. He must reproduce within himself the mysteries of Christ, chiefly the Incarnation, the childhood, the Crucifixion, the death, the burial, the Resurrection, and the Ascension. This doctrine is not new. It is based on the teaching of St. Paul: "With Christ I am nailed to the cross. And I live, now not I: but Christ liveth in me." [14] "A faithful saying: for if we be dead with Him, we shall live also with Him." [15] "Buried with Him [Christ] in baptism: in whom also you are risen by the faith of the operation of God." [16] "Therefore, if you be risen with Christ, seek the things that are above, where Christ is sitting at the right hand of God. . . . For you are dead: and your life is hid with Christ in God." [17] This is Pauline Christianity, every Christian a saint, another Christ, every Christian, without exception, obliged to follow Christ, once he has been "buried together with Him by baptism into death." Out of the waters of baptism the Christian has risen to a new life, like Christ who arose from the dead: "That as Christ is risen from the dead by the glory of the Father, so we

---

[13] Head of this French School was Pierre de Bérulle (1575–1629), founder of the Oratory in France. His disciples were Condren, St. Vincent de Paul, Olier, St. John Eudes, Blessed Grignon de Montfort. Bossuet must be numbered also among his disciples.

[14] Gal. 2:19 f.

[15] II Tim. 2:11.

[16] Col. 2:12.

[17] Col. 3:1, 3.

also may walk in newness of life. For if we have been planted together in the likeness of His death, we shall be also in the likeness of His Resurrection." [18] If every baptized Christian must so imitate Christ in his own life as to be a faithful image of Christ Himself, another Christ, how can any Christian be dispensed from the obligation of tending to perfection?

237. The teaching of the Fathers on this point is nothing more than a comment on the words of St. Paul, insisting on the universal obligation for all Christians to imitate God, to follow Christ: "Christianity is an imitation of the divine nature." [19] "What else," asks the same St. Gregory of Nyssa, "must he do who has been made worthy to bear the glorious surname of Christ [Christian], but to examine diligently all his thoughts, words, and deeds, and see whether each one of them is leading to Christ or away from Him." [20] In his *Paedagogus,* Clement of Alexandria exhorts the true Gnostic, who is the common Christian, to fulfill the will of the heavenly Father by imitating our Savior: "Let us, O children of the good Father—nurslings of the good Paedagogus—fulfill the Father's will, listen to the Word, and take on the heavenly mode of life of our Savior; and meditating on the heavenly mode of life according to which we have been deified, let us anoint ourselves with the perennial immortal bloom of gladness —that anointment of sweet fragrance—having a clear example of immortality in the walk and conversation of the Lord; and following the footsteps of God." [21]

St. John Chrysostom commenting on the words of St.

[18] Rom. 6:4 f.
[19] St. Gregory of Nyssa, *De professione Christiana.*
[20] *Idem, De perfecta Christiani forma.*
[21] Clement of Alexandria, *Paedagogus,* I, 12.

Paul: "Be ye followers of me, as I also am of Christ," [22] says: "This is the rule of a most perfect Christianity." [23] Yet, this rule becomes a necessary rule of conduct for every one of Christ's disciples, because every disciple of Christ, every Christian, must take up his cross and follow the divine Master. Anyone who either refuses or neglects this sacred duty of following the Master, is not worthy of Him, not worthy of the Christian name.

238. Some authors, like Cardinal Vives in his *Compendium theologiae ascetico-mysticae,* distinguish between a lower (*infima*), a middle (*media*), and a higher (*superior*) perfection. The first excludes only mortal sins, the second excludes also deliberate venial sins, the third includes the keeping of the counsels according to one's condition and state in life. The counsels contribute to the avoidance of imperfections, and consequently to the avoidance of venial sins, because imperfections dispose the soul to commit venial sins.[24] According to these authors, all men are obliged to tend to the lower and middle perfection but not to the higher perfection, which alone deserves the name of perfection.[25] We consider this distinction rather confusing. Perfection is one. We cannot speak of three different perfections of the spiritual life without contradicting the very concept of perfection. It is, therefore, more advisable to speak of three stages or degrees of perfection. This is in accordance with what we have stated and proved in earlier chapters, namely, that spiritual perfection in this life is relative and progres-

---

[22] I Cor. 11:1.

[23] *In Epist. ad Cor., Hom.,* 25, 3.

[24] I. C. Card. Vives, *Compendium theologiae ascetico-mysticae,* Rome, 1907, pp. 55 ff.

[25] *Perfectio proprie dicta, seu stricte talis, sive superior, non obligat omnes homines. Ibid.,* p. 56.

sive. All men are obliged to tend to perfection, to the one and the same kind of Christian perfection, but each one according to his vocation, state in life, grace of God, personal fervor.

239. One may remain all his life in the initial stage, or first degree, keeping the commandments, avoiding mortal sins, wishing, but not seriously and efficiently, for higher perfection. Another will go one step further in conquering himself and will avoid also deliberate venial sins. This is not a different kind of Christian perfection, but it differs from the first only in degree. The first was the essential, incipient perfection, the second is a more advanced or proficient stage of that same perfection. Nor is the so-called higher perfection different from the preceding one. The avoidance of imperfections is only a higher degree of the same perfection, not a different kind. The authors mentioned above do not speak here of the evangelical counsels as kept, under vows, in the religious state, but as observed in part at least or in spirit by any Christian, even outside the religious state.[26] We maintain that this higher perfection is for all Christians, and that every Christian should tend to it. It is the perfection preached by Christ and His apostles. It is the perfection St. Paul demanded from the common faithful: "All whatsoever you do in word or in work, do all in the name of the Lord Jesus Christ, giving thanks to God and to the Father by Him. . . . Whatsoever you do, do it from the heart, as to the Lord, and not to men." [27] This is, no doubt, a Christian higher perfection, a perfection tending to the avoid-

[26] *Consilia autem quorum observantia requiritur ad perfectionem proprie talem, sunt illa quae propriae uniuscuiusque conditioni sunt proportionata. Ibid.*, p. 55.
[27] Col. 3:17, 23.

ance of deliberate imperfections. It is preached to all because it should be the goal of every Christian.

240. Some authors have tried to prove their assertion that not all Christians are called to the higher perfection by quoting Mark 10:17–27, and interpreting the answer of Christ to the young man, in the sense that the common faithful in the world are called simply to observe the commandments in order to enter eternal life, whereas to be perfect one must leave the world and follow Christ by actual observance of the counsels *in re* and not merely in spirit. The real meaning of the answer of Christ to that young Jew was that, to possess eternal life, it was enough for him to keep the commandments of the Old Law, which was still binding (a law Christ had not come to suppress but to fulfill); but, if he wished to be perfect, he had to embrace Christianity, by renouncing his possessions and following Christ. The fact that Christ demanded from that young man that he sell everything he had and give it to the poor, as a requirement for Christian perfection, does not prove that Christian higher perfection can be attained only by those who profess actual poverty, or any other of the evangelical counsels. The Lord demands detachment from everything, so that His disciples may put all their trust in Him and not in their possessions. Detachment and renunciation in this sense are necessary for Christian perfection in general. Not the possession of riches but the attachment to riches, the trust in them, constitutes a real obstacle to perfection and often even to salvation: "How hard is it for them that trust in riches, to enter into the kingdom of God?" [28]

241. This is the interpretation given to Mark 10:17–27

[28] Mark 10:24.

by Clement of Alexandria in a celebrated work of his.[29]
"He [Christ] does not, as some conceive off-hand, bid him
throw away the substance he possessed, and abandon his
property; but bids him banish from his soul his notions
about wealth, his excitement and morbid feeling about
it, the anxieties, which are the thorns of existence, which
choke the seed of life. . . . If no one had anything, what
room would be left among men for giving? And how can
this dogma fail to be found plainly opposed to and con-
flicting with many other excellent teachings of the Lord?
. . . The renunciation, then, and selling of all possessions,
is to be understood as spoken of the passions of the soul." [30]
The Christian perfection of the counsels does not consist
in the fact that a person does not possess anything, that
he is unmarried, and subject to authority. It consists first
of all in the will, which must offer itself without any
encumbrance to the cause of Christ, to the service of God.
The spirit of the counsels, therefore, is required and is
sufficient for Christian perfection, even for the highest
perfection, such as was reached by a St. Louis IX, king
of France (of whom even a Voltaire said: "Never has it
been accorded to man to push virtue further"), or by a
St. Elizabeth of Hungary, a king's daughter and later wife
of the Landgrave of Thuringia, or by the other St. Elizabeth, queen of Portugal. The actual exterior renunciation
of all things for Christ's sake is a matter of counsel in the
way of Christian perfection; the interior renunciation
is a necessary condition and, therefore, it is obligatory
for all those who strive after Christian perfection.

The actual exterior renunciation is a necessary prereq-

[29] Clement of Alexandria, *Who Is the Rich Man That Shall Be Saved?*
[30] *Ibid.*, 11, 13, 14.

uisite in the state of perfection, called the religious state, which we shall speak of in the following chapter. The perfection we have considered in the present chapter is personal and interior; the obligation of tending to it is also personal and interior regardless of the exterior condition or state in life of the individual.

CHAPTER XIX

THE STATE OF PERFECTION

242. Perfection itself is something personal and interior, the state of perfection is an institution offering all the facilities for the acquisition and practice of perfection. The state of perfection, therefore, is something exterior to the soul. It must be not understood as a state or condition of the soul, like the state of grace, or the state of sin. One who is in the state of grace actually possesses divine grace, but one who is in the state of perfection may or may not possess perfection. All he possesses is a grand opportunity with all necessary means for acquiring perfection.

243. The given description of the state of perfection applies only to one of them, namely, the religious state, which is known as the state for acquiring perfection, *status perfectionis acquirendae,* or simply as a school perfection. However, no one ever graduates from this school during his life, because his work is never entirely completed. All spiritual perfection is always progressive, always relative, never absolute and complete. Graduation day for everyone in the school of perfection is the day of death and judgment. There is also a state of acquired perfection, *status perfectionis acquisitae,* that of the bishops, and one of ministry, *status perfectionis exercendae,* that of priests with or without care of souls. We are mainly concerned with the first one, namely, the religious state.

244. The religious state as a state of perfection is thus defined by the Code of Canon Law: "A permanent manner of living in community wherein the faithful, in addition to those things that are of precept, engage themselves by vow to observe the evangelical counsels of obedience, chastity, and poverty." [1]

"One is said to be in the state of perfection," says St. Thomas, "not through having the act of perfect charity, but through binding himself in perpetuity and with a certain solemnity to those things that pertain to perfection. Moreover it happens that some persons bind themselves to that which they do not keep, and some fulfill that to which they have not bound themselves." [2] The last observation made by the Angelic Doctor should warn us against the danger of mistaking the state of perfection for perfection itself, and concluding that no one can attain perfection outside the state of perfection. The perfection that religious strive after is not different from the ordinary Christian perfection except in the extrinsic form of tending to it. The extrinsic form consists in living in community according to a permanent rule approved by the Church, but especially in binding oneself by vow to observe the evangelical counsels of obedience, chastity, and poverty.

245. Living under a rule and under the vow of obedience, both intended to guide a person to perfection and sanctity, means to acquire a certain stability or stable condition in one's mode of life. The work of perfection is subtracted from the inconstancy of a free form of living and becomes a state of life, the state of perfection. The

[1] Canon 487.
[2] *Summa theol.*, IIa IIae, q. 184, a. 4.

actual removal of many and various obstacles by the profession of the evangelical counsels, the enlightening guidance of the rule, the experienced assistance and direction
of superiors, the constant good example of other members
of the religious community, make of religious life a school
of perfection.

246. Christian perfection is a masterpiece of divine
grace and human diligence and ingenuity. It is an art and
a science. If for human arts and sciences we have schools
and academies, why should there not be a school for the
learning of the science of the saints, an academy for acquiring the art of arts? The Church of Christ, as a perfect
society, containing within itself all the means necessary
for the attainment of its end, could not lack an institution
of this kind, a school of perfection. The religious state is
this school.

247. To affirm that the religious state is either of divine
or ecclesiastical origin would be not only historically false
but also theologically exaggerated. It is based on the
teaching and the example of Christ and has, at all times,
received the approval, the encouragement, and the pro-
tection of the Church.

The bitter feelings of John Wyclif against all religious
people are well known. His errors were condemned in the
general council of Constance, 1418. Wyclif had asserted
that anyone entering a religious community would become less capable and fit for the observance of the commandments of God; that the saints who had established
the religious orders in the Church had sinned by so doing;
that the religious themselves could no longer be considered Christians like the rest.[3] Those who abjured

[3] Denz., 601, 602, 603, 624.

Wyclif's errors were requested to answer thirty-nine questions. One of them regarded the religious life: "Whether
he believed that the religious orders approved by the
Church had been properly and righly introduced by their
saintly founders." [4] We have here an official statement
about the origin of religious communities. Great saints,
Sancti Patres, by their personal initiative had accepted
and formed disciples according to their own saintly mode
of life. After ample evidence had been offered by such
religious families of their sincerity and sanctity of purpose
and of their usefulness in Christian society, the Church
approved them. All of them had their beginning in the
personal perfection of their saintly founders, a perfection
ordinarily acquired outside the state of perfection.

248. Personal striving after perfection, intrinsic sanctity, have no substitutes. The state of perfection cannot
take their place. It is there to encourage, to help, to ex-
pedite every personal effort toward perfection, not to
offer the mere name and the approved uniform of it. The
general obligation of tending to perfection is not substi-
tuted by another obligation, in making religious profession, but it is merely increased by a new one, that of the
new state: "Each and every religious superior as well as
subject is bound to tend toward the perfection of his
state." [5] This new duty is fulfilled by obeying the rule
and keeping the vows.

249. The way of perfection remains essentially the
same even in the state of perfection. A religious must go
through the purgative and the illuminative way before
reaching the relative perfection of the unitive way: "All

[4] Denz., 680.
[5] *Code of Canon Law,* can. 593.

are not perfect in religion, but some are beginners, some proficient." [6] Therefore it is necessary for a religious to be well instructed in ascetical theology. Ordinarily they receive a thorough explanation of their vows and rule, but often only a superficial and fragmentary introduction in ascetical and mystical theology. Some of them do not know any form of mental prayer besides meditation. The impression prevails that mystical graces are dangerous for both the individual and the community. The consequence is that many are retarded or hindered in their spiritual advancement. The position of the religious who has been favored with extraordinary graces becomes very delicate. A well-enlightened community is better disposed toward mystical phenomena and higher forms of mental prayer.

250. The religious life is not only a school of Christian perfection but also a calm port where the human mind, out of the stormy sea of the secular life, finds quiet and peace from outward solicitudes. These solicitudes are of three kinds: the attachment to external goods, the love and concupiscence of bodily satisfactions, the inordinate attachment to the freedom of our spirit. The three religious vows remove the source of this threefold solicitude. Lastly, religious life is also a holocaust whereby a man offers himself and his possessions entirely to God.[7] This doctrine of the Angelic Doctor has been confirmed more recently by Pope Pius XI in his Apostolic Letter to the general superiors of religious orders.[8] The idea of com-

---

[6] St. Thomas, *Summa theol.*, IIa IIae, q. 186, a. 1.

[7] Cf. *ibid.*, a. 7.

[8] *Acta Ap. Sedis*, 1924, p. 133. *Eiusmodi autem consilia quicumque, obligata Deo fide, servaturum se spondeat, is non modo exsolvitur impedimentis quae mortales a sanctitate remorari solent, ut bona fortunae, ut coniugii curae*

plete surrender of our will, through the vow of obedience, is essential to the state of perfection and to religious life. Obedience is the oldest and the most comprehensive form of religious profession. Continence and poverty can be observed also in the world, and a person does not thereby become a religious. Obedience to the rule and to religious superiors completes the oblation and makes it a holocaust. In the early centuries the vow of virginity was considered the equivalent of martyrdom. How much more is this true of religious profession? We take for granted that charity or other higher motives compel a person to embrace the religious state. The Lord has promised a hundredfold in return, even in this life, to those who have abandoned everything and have followed Him.[9] If anyone enters the religious life merely to escape the responsibilities and the many cares of living in the world and to enjoy in peace the promised earthly hundredfold, he will never make great strides on the way of Christian perfection. He cannot serve as an example to seculars, as every religious should. Many purely secular activities, undertaken with holy intentions by modern religious communities, their almost continual association with secular persons, their living outside the community for long periods of time, are the common cause why so little progress is made in perfection, why discipline breaks down, religious spirit disappears, and charity grows cold. There is nothing sadder than a religious community that remains without concern on such a low level of spiritual-

---

sollicitudinesque, ut immoderata rerum omnium libertas; sed etiam tam recto expeditoque itinere ad perfectionem vitae progreditur, ut iamiam in salutis portu anchoram veluti iecisse videatur.

[9] Matt. 19:29.

ity. It becomes a school in which nobody teaches or nobody cares to learn. Some fervor and some progress in spiritual life, no matter how slow and how little, are essential to the welfare of the community as well as to the individual religious person.

251. Bishops are in the state of perfection which is called *status perfectionis acquisitae*. The stability of their office, the fullness of their priesthood, the fact that they are spiritual fathers to everyone in their jurisdiction, including priests and religious, give bishops the firmness of a state in life, the superiority of acquired perfection. According to St. Thomas' view, the state of perfection of bishops is more excellent than that of the religious state because "bishops are those who make others perfect, religious are made perfect." [10] Furthermore, no other ecclesiastical order has given such a large number of saints to the Church of God as the order of bishops. The personal holiness of so many great prelates shows that the perfection of their state is not merely extrinsic.

One may cavil by saying that the larger number of saints among the bishops is explained by the fact that candidates to that high office are chosen ordinarily from the best and most worthy of the clergy. To this we may reply that, because the exalted office of bishops is a state of perfection, it was possible even for the most worthy candidates not only to remain such but to advance to a much higher perfection and to consummate sanctity.

252. We come now to a consideration of priests and sacred ministers. Are they in a state of perfection? St. Thomas says that priests and deacons are not in a state

[10] St. Thomas, *Summa theol.*, IIa IIae, q.184, a.7.

of perfection, although he requires an inward perfection.[11] The reason for his view seems not convincing: "By receiving a certain order a man receives the power of exercising certain sacred acts, but he is not bound on this account to things pertaining to perfection, except so far as in the Western Church the receiving of a sacred order includes the taking of a vow of continence, which is one of the things pertaining to perfection." [12] Evidently the Angelic Doctor speaks here only of the outward perfection, or the state or perfection, for he expressly admits, toward the middle of the same article, the obligation for inward perfection: "Therefore it is clear that from the fact that a man receives a sacred order he is not placed simply in the state of perfection, although inward perfection is required in order that one exercise such acts worthily."

253. Considering the nature of sacred orders and the nature of a state, as explained by St. Thomas himself, we should not hesitate to conclude that every man in sacred orders, especially a priest, is in a state of perfection, which may be called *status perfectionis exercendae*.

Let us see what St. Thomas means by the word "state." He says: "State, properly speaking, denotes a kind of position whereby a thing is disposed with a certain immobility in a manner according with its nature. . . . Consequently matters which easily change and are extrinsic to them do not constitute a state among men, for instance, that a man be rich or poor, of high or low rank. . . . But that alone seemingly pertains to a man's state, which regards an obligation binding his person, so far, namely, as

[11] *Ibid.*, a.6.
[12] *Ibid.*

a man is his own master or subject to another. Therefore state properly regards freedom or servitude whether in spiritual or in civil matters." [13]

A state, therefore, implies stability, a binding obligation, freedom or servitude. We find these elements present in persons who are in sacred orders. Hence we maintain that they are in a state of perfection.

254. Clerics are so called from the Greek word *kleros*, because by their dedication and consecration to the service of God and His Church, they become the "lot" or "inheritance" of the Lord. In the major orders this dedication becomes permanent. The sacramental character of the sacred orders, the solemn vow of continence or celibacy, the grave obligation, for life, to recite the canonical hours, the promise of obedience made by the new *presbyter* to the ordaining bishop, are more than ordinary elements of stability, more than binding obligations, more than evident marks of spiritual servitude or divine service.

The mind of the Church in this respect appears from the words of the *Pontificale Romanum:* "If you receive this order (of subdeacon), *you will no longer be at liberty* to recede from your resolution, but *you will be obliged to serve God perpetually,* to serve whom is to reign." [14] The italics are ours. They stress the conditions required by St. Thomas in order that a condition in life may be called a state. They are all present.

It is a state of perfection, not of acquired perfection, like that much higher of the bishops, but of perfection of ministry or service, *status perfectionis exercendae.* The service of God ought to be the most perfect service a

[13] *Ibid.,* q. 183, a. 1.
[14] Ordination of subdeacons.

creature, human or angelic, ever performs. To be dedicated and consecrated permanently and irrevocably to
such a service means to be in a state of perfection which
is midway between the state of perfection of the religious
and that of the bishops and other higher prelates.

255. Marriage is a state because of its indissolubility,
the stability of the sacramental contract. Should the sacrament of holy orders produce a lesser effect of stability,
when we know that not even death, which dissolves the
bond of matrimony, can erase from the soul of the or-
dained priest the indelible character of the sacrament?
Besides, the service of the altar and the care of souls de-
mand not only inward sanctity but also outward decorum
and perfection. This the Church expects from her ministers: "Take care that you may illustrate the gospel by
your living works," the *Pontificale* exhorts the deacons,
"to those to whom you announce it with your lips." To the
priests, the same *Pontificale* says: "Bear in mind what you
do. Let your conduct be in conformity with the action you
perform." The priest is an ambassador of Christ, another
Christ. Inward and outward perfection are a sacred duty
for every priest. The Church requires that clerics as a
class lead also outwardly a life that is holier than that of
the laity. This fact implies a state of perfection: "Clerics
must lead an interior and exterior life holier than that of
the laity and give these the good example of virtue and
good works." [15]

[15] *Code of Canon Law,* can. 124.

CHAPTER XX

SPIRITUAL READING AND MEDITATION,
THE PARTICULAR EXAMEN

256. The nature and purpose of meditation and spiritual reading have been explained. These two means of perfection are now analyzed again, but only in their mutual relation. From this comparative study, a more comprehensive knowledge of the method to be followed in discursive prayer will be acquired.

Spiritual reading, meditation, devout prayer, are links of one chain, rungs of one ladder, three tones of the same chord, a perfect triad. Each of them is a perfect instrument, the three combined produce a spiritual harmony.

Prayer, vocal and mental, is the heavenly accompaniment to spiritual reading and meditation; it is the melodic counterpoint of the word read in a pious book or spoken internally by the mind in devout and deep reflections. Prayer is an essential part of meditation. Without prayer, meditation is nothing but a study. Prayer, as the raising of mind and heart to God, is also a part of spiritual reading; not an essential part, however, but only an accidental one, a quality. Without this quality, spiritual reading is merely a reading and nothing else. We read for spiritual instruction and edification. The subject of our reading becomes food for our soul. The mind must first digest this food that the soul may assimilate it. In spiritual reading the process of digestion is a simple one. It consists in grasping the significance of what we read together with some obvious application to our present needs. Here and there the heart is stirred to pious affections, and good resolutions of a general nature begin to take shape in our will.

257. From this brief analysis, it appears that spiritual reading is the mother of meditation. The Latin word *meditatio* means first of all a careful reading, a study. It was used in this sense by spiritual writers for many centuries before it received the well-defined meaning of discursive mental prayer. The methodical form of meditation, that has been in use since the Middle Ages, may be considered an evolution or development of the pious and careful reading of the Sacred Scripture universally practiced by the early Christians. Spiritual reading is the ordinary companion of meditation. A beginner in discursive prayer needs a book for his meditation. He must read carefully before reflections are made, resolutions taken, and prayers formulated. Spiritual reading leads ordinarily to meditation and occasionally to even higher forms of mental prayer.

258. It may seem strange that St. Theresa, who was raised to the most sublime degrees of mystical contemplation, found meditation difficult in the beginning of her religious life and had to resort to reading a book in order to elevate her mind to God: "God never endowed me with the gift of making reflections with my mind, or with that of using the imagination to any good purpose. My imagination is so sluggish, that even if I would think of, or picture to myself, as I used to try to picture, our Lord's Humanity, I never could do it. . . . Reading is of great service towards procuring recollection in any one who proceeds in this way, and it is even necessary for him, however little may be that he reads, if only as a substitute for the mental prayer which is beyond his reach." [1]

The case of St. Theresa is rather common in our dynamic age. A person may be unable to perform discursive prayer or picture to himself anything at all on account of congenital weakness of intellect or infirmity or vocational distraction and fatigue. A pious reading, as described above, may in similar cases take the place of meditation. As a substitute for meditation, it is no longer a mere reading, it is a simplified mental prayer. "This method of praying, in which the understanding makes no reflections, has this property: the soul must gain much, or lose. I mean, that those who advance without meditation, make great progress, because it is done by love. But to attain to this involves great labour, except to those persons whom it is our Lord's good pleasure to lead quickly to the prayer of quiet. I know of some. For those who walk in this way, a book is profitable, that by the help thereof they may more quickly recollect themselves." [2] "It is likewise an excellent thing to take a good book in your own language, in order to recollect the thoughts, that so you pray well vocally." [3] Spiritual reading is, therefore, the mother of meditation, the sister of vocal prayer.

259. The word of God is a light on the way of perfection: "Thy word is a lamp to my feet, and a light to my paths." [4] As long as this light remains sealed in a book, it is a light under a bushel. The reading of the word of God puts that light on a candlestick "that it may shine to all

[1] St. Theresa, *Life*, chap. 4.
[2] *Ibid.*, chap. 9.
[3] *The Way of Perfection*, chap. 26.
[4] Ps. 118:105.

that are in the house." [5] It shines, then, to all in the house
of the reader's soul, to his mind, his heart, his imagination, his will. The Sacred Scriptures and, in proportion,
every good book harmonize fully with every mood and
state of the human soul. They send forth a ray of light in
the heart of the repentant sinner, a ray of comfort in the
soul of the afflicted, a flood of light and peace in the heart
that is pure and humble, a living flame in the heart of the
apostle. They sound a serious warning to the heedless, a
cheering word to the disheartened. The same word may
ring at times like the voice of a father, at other times like
that of a judge, at others like that of a brother or a friend.

260. Augustine had more than once rested his eyes on
that famous passage of the Epistles of St. Paul that
brought about his conversion, but never before had his
soul been in such a receptive mood as on that day of July,
386, in Milan, after the visit of his friend Ponticianus and
after hearing the mysterious voice: "Take up and read;
Take up and read." [6] He opened the volume of the Epistles of St. Paul, a copy of which he kept always at hand,
and in silence he read that passage on which his eyes first
fell. He read the word he had needed always, the word
he had read often before. He read, and his soul was
flooded with divine light; he saw himself and blushed.
He cried to God, and the lifelong hold of lust upon his
soul was finally broken. From that moment on, Augustine
was a new man, a Christian at heart, potentially a saint,
a major luminary of the Church of Christ. That short reading had been more than meditation or contemplation, it
had been a clear vision of truth of an extraordinary, mys-

[5] Matt. 5:15.
[6] St. Augustine, *Confessions*, VIII, 12.

tical nature. This is not the only instance that a reading
of the Scripture brought about a radical change in a
person's life. The reading, however, is only an instrument,
an opportunity for divine Providence to perform such
works of grace. To better dispose the soul for similar
works of grace, spiritual reading should be preceded and
followed by a short prayer, in which the reader asks the
divine Majesty for the Spirit of wisdom and understanding.

261. With regard to the daily amount of spiritual reading, St. Jerome, one of the great readers of all times, seems
unwilling to assign any other limit to the reading of the
Scriptures except such as imposed by fatigue. So he writes
to the virgin Eustochium: "Read often, learn all you can.
Let sleep overcome you, the book still in your hand; when
your head falls, let it be on the sacred page." [7] Lest sleep
and exhaustion come too soon, he requires that a definite
number of verses from Holy Scripture be read every day
before reading anything else: "When you eat your meals,
think that you must immediately afterward pray and
read. Have a fixed number of lines of Holy Scripture, and
render it as your task to your Lord. On no account resign
yourself to sleep until you filled the basket of your breast
with a woof of this weaving. After the Holy Scriptures you
should read the writings of learned men; of those at any
rate whose faith is well known. You need not go into the
mire to seek for gold." [8] Such is St. Jerome's advice and
direction for selective spiritual reading.

262. Pelagius, a contemporary of St. Jerome, advices
moderation in spiritual reading: "Let your reading be

[7] *Epist.*, 22, 17.
[8] *Epist.*, 54, 11.

moderate; let your prudence and not your fatigue put a limit to it." [9] We have said before that spiritual reading must offer spiritual food to heart and mind, but all kinds of food must be taken with moderation to be beneficial. Too much and too long reading cannot be easily assimilated by the spirit. St. Jerome himself is for moderation in spiritual reading when he assigns a definite number of verses of Scripture as a daily task. When he advises Eustochium to read until sleep overcomes her, it is a question only of optional reading during her leisure hours, of filling her soul with sacred thoughts before going to sleep so that her head may "fall on the sacred page."

263. The mutual relation between spiritual reading and meditation is expressed by St. Ambrose when he says we must meditate on what we have read in order that we may imitate it: "Let the daily reading be our exercise, in order that we may meditate to follow what we have read." [10] He considers this exercise of spiritual reading as a training which makes the soul strong and ready to meet and overcome the enemy in time of temptation. Reading and meditating are two terms expressing often the same idea in St. Ambrose and contemporary writers, but it is always a careful reading accompanied by reflection: "Meditate, therefore, all day long on the law; but your reading must not be hasty and perfunctory." [11]

264. St. Isidore of Seville analyzes spiritual reading in relation to both mental and vocal prayer, pointing out its many blessings: "By means of prayers we are cleansed, by means of reading we are instructed. . . . Whoever

[9] *Ad Demetriadem*, 23.
[10] *Exposit. in Ps.* 118.
[11] *Ibid.*, XIII, 17.

wishes to be always with God, must pray often and read often. For when we pray, we ourselves speak to God; but when we read, God speaks to us. All [spiritual] progress comes from spiritual reading and meditation, for by reading we learn what we did not know, by meditations we preserve what we have learnt." [12]

THE PARTICULAR EXAMEN

265. The examination of conscience is essentially an exercise of the practical spiritual life. Its purpose is self-knowledge and moral improvement. Without a perfect self-knowledge, no advancement in spiritual life, no perfection, can be hoped for. There is a general examination of conscience known to all Christians who go regularly to confession. The general examination is a daily exercise of the ascetical life. Its practice is as old as the human desire for perfection. For us Christians, it is more than a mere checking of our spiritual status or condition. It implies real sorrow for sins committed and a firm resolution of amendment. It is not our purpose to explain further this well-known exercise. There is, however, another examination of conscience, known as the particular examen, the practical side of which has been explained before. According to St. Ignatius Loyola, the particular examination of conscience is as important as meditation itself in freeing the soul from sin and furthering its progress in virtue. In some respects, the particular examen is even more important than meditation because it is more specific, more personal. Meditation is based on principles, the particular examen on facts. In meditation, our entire conduct is analyzed under the light of truths just then con-

[12] *Sent.,* III, 8.

sidered; in particular examen, one specific fault is singled out in our conduct and is run down relentlessly until eliminated. When the negative part, the rooting out of a fault, has been completed, the positive part, the planting of the opposite virtue in place of the former fault, is undertaken with the same determination and on the same plan. When, for example, pride and vainglory have been eliminated, humility will become the subject of particular examination. It is like planting a Christian trophy on the grave of sin.

266. The old strategy of dividing the enemy brings the same good results with inward as with outward enemies. The predominant fault is the first to be singled out as the subject of the particular examen. Its exterior manifestations should be curbed first, for they are often a cause of bad example and scandal. Whatever remains of it in our thoughts and feelings should be curbed next. While we seem to direct our attention to one thing at a time, many other virtues are practiced, for instance, mortification, humility, devotion, charity. That all our efforts in the practice of particular examination may be effective, they must be accompanied by prayer, which puts the seal of spirituality and of the supernatural on all ascetical exercises.

267. The method of marking down in a notebook twice daily the number of faults committed, was introduced by St. Ignatius Loyola, who gives a detailed explanation of it in his *Spiritual Exercises*. This practice has a deep psychological significance. A written confession, an admission of guilt, is an indictment against self-love. The custom of writing down one's own faults, for the purpose of amendment, is very old, antedating St. Ignatius. St.

Athanasius writes that this practice was suggested by the great St. Anthony to his disciples: "That one may avoid sin, the following should be observed: Let each of us mark and write down our actions and the motions of our soul as if to show them to others. Believe me, it will happen that because we are ashamed of being discovered by other people, we will stop committing sin and entertaining evil thoughts." [13]

268. In this examen, as in other ascetical exercises, constancy and perseverance are of primary importance for success. There will always be room for improvement throughout this mortal life, even for saints. It is related that St. Ignatius Loyola remained loyal to the practice of marking down the result of his particular examen in the little notebook until the end of his life. The last entry was made the day before he died.

269. The faults of one kind may be divided or classified according to their gravity as serious faults (*peccata*), deliberate venial sins (*offensiones*), indeliberate venial sins and imperfections (*negligentiae*).[14] When, by the grace of God and the habitual practice of the particular examen, serious faults have been overcome, the examen will have to continue on the same subject in order to eradicate deliberate venial offenses in words, actions, thoughts, omissions. Next come the negligences or imperfections. Imperfections open a wide field of action for the particular examen. We must distinguish, however, between imperfections that can and should be eliminated from the soul and such as will remain with us in spite of

[13] St. Athanasius, *Vita S. Antonii,* 58.
[14] This classification is taken from the Oblation Prayer of the Mass, *Suscipe Sancte Pater . . . pro innumerabilibus peccatis, et offensionibus, et negligentiis meis.*

all diligence and perfection of charity acquired. Imperfections of the first kind are caused by some remnants of emotions and attachments not fully mortified; the others are owing entirely to the limitations and natural frailties of human nature, like feeling the effects of fatigue, involuntary distractions. The former are involuntary venial sins; they can and should be made the subject of particular examination. It would be waste of time to institute a particular examen on the second kind of imperfections. Only a special grace of God can deliver us from such frailties. They have their own purpose in spiritual life, providing motives for humility, fear, and trust in God.

CHAPTER XXI

ASCETICISM AND MYSTICISM,
QUIETISM

270. The nature of asceticism has been sufficiently explained in this volume. Mysticism enters only indirectly in the ascetical Christian life. The proper place for its consideration is in mystical theology. The specific natures of asceticism and of mysticism will now be compared that we may better define the proper scope and domain of each in spiritual life. The whole range of spiritual life is penetrated by a mystical element, divine grace. Asceticism must have this mystical element in order to be a Christian asceticism; without it, asceticism would be nothing more than a kind of Stoicism. However, mysticism is something more than divine grace, which is the common divine element of Christian asceticism and mysticism.

271. What is mysticism? In the strict sense of the word, mysticism is an experimental knowledge of God and union with Him, ordinarily granted and experienced in infused contemplation. True mysticism begins, therefore, with infused contemplation. All other phenomena that may accompany or follow infused contemplation are only accidental, non-essential parts of mysticism. The experimental knowledge of God's presence, a soul's experience of the supernatural and the divine, and the most profound "awareness" of God, are the essence of mysticism. Infused contemplation is in contrast to acquired contemplation. Acquired contemplation is the most sublime form of mental prayer of the ascetical life. Infused contemplation, in various degrees of perfection, is the mental prayer of the mystical life. Mystical life begins with infused contemplation. Infused contemplation is a gift of God and not the result of our diligence and activity. The soul is not the efficient cause of infused contemplation, but merely its recipient. With mysticism, a state of relative passivity is introduced, but only with regard to contemplation. In every other activity of the soul, nothing is changed. On the contrary, the works of charity, of apostolic zeal, are rather increased. It is not the supine passivity of the Quietists, which means inactivity. Except for the time of contemplation, the mystic continues his ascetical practices as usual, even perhaps with more fervor than before. It is a well-known fact that great mystics have always been the most active and ardent apostles of Christianity. Only false mysticism produces inactivity.

272. The relative passivity of the soul in contemplation is, nevertheless, so characteristic of the mystical state, so new and extraordinary, that it can be regarded as the line of demarcation between asceticism and mysticism, or as the criterion for distinguishing between infused and acquired contemplation.

273. Mysticism has been defined, at times, as the knowledge of God by love, in opposition to the natural or philosophical knowledge of God by reason, and the common supernatural knowledge by faith. A knowledge of God by love is an experimental knowledge. This definition is strikingly mystical. It reminds us of the *amo ut intelligam* of the mystics of the early Middle Ages, not in opposition to but in addition to the *credo ut intelligam* of

the Scholastics. To exclude misunderstandings, this second definition of mysticism must be explained. What does it mean to know God by love? Love is naturally only an effect, not a cause of knowledge. Love is an act of the will, and our will is not a cognitive power. It is understood that we speak here only of rational love. Likewise, in the supernatural order, it is faith, not charity, that is the principle of supernatural knowledge.

274. Is it, perhaps, an exaggeration or a misconception to say that mysticism is a knowledge of God by love? There is enough ground of truth to justify this definition. In infused contemplation, God's presence is felt in the center of the soul [1] without the slightest effort on the side of the human cognitive power, at the same time that a great love of God is being experienced as a great reality. God is known, and His love is experienced, without the ordinary process of our intellectual faculty; hence the conclusion is evident, that God is known experimentally by love. Even for the mystic, in the present life, every knowledge of God is by faith: "We see now through a glass in a dark manner; but then face to face. Now I know in part; but then I shall know even as I am known. And now there remain faith, hope, and charity, these three." [2] The "now" is the present life, the "then" is the blessed future life. The more or less obscure knowledge of faith becomes no clear vision in mysticism. Mystical knowledge imparts a firmer conviction but not always a clearer one. The dark night of the senses and the dark night of the spirit which, according to St. John of the Cross, form

---

[1] Christian and non-Christian mystics agree that the mystical knowledge does not take place in one or the other faculty of the soul but in its very substance. Cf. Plotinus, *Ennead.*, VI, 9, 8.

[2] I Cor. 13:12 f.

such a large portion of the mystical life, do not indicate a clear knowledge: "It is now, I think, becoming clear how faith is a dark night to the soul, and how the soul likewise must be dark, or in darkness as to its own light, so that it may allow itself to be guided by faith to this high goal of [mystical] union. But, in order that the soul may be able to do this, it will now be well to continue describing, in somewhat greater detail, this darkness which the soul must have, in order that it may enter into this abyss of faith." [3] We should note that St. John of the Cross speaks here only of faith as a principle of supernatural knowledge. Pseudo-Dionysius speaks of this mystical darkness which is otherwise most resplendent: "A darkness that shines brighter than light, that invisibly and intangibly illuminates with splendours of inconceivable beauty the soul that sees not." [4] A friend who in absolute darkness comes to us, speaks with us, gives us his hand, offers us tangible proofs of his presence even if we do not see him on account of darkness. Some authors think that the mystics' experimental knowledge of God is something like meeting a well-known and very dear friend in the dark.

275. The mysticism just described is the equivalent of mystical theology, or mysticism in the strict sense of the word. This mysticism has nothing to do with asceticism proper, just as infused contemplation has nothing to do with acquired contemplation. The object, however, is one for all, namely, God and the union of the soul with Him through love. The manner is different. Mysticism in the wide sense of the word means a divine, secret element,

[3] St. John of the Cross, *Subida del Monte Carmelo*, II, 4, 1.
[4] *Mystical Theology*, I.

such as divine grace. This element is common to asceticism and mysticism. It was on account of this common mystical element that the whole range of spiritual life, asceticism and mysticism, was for a long time called simply mystical theology. For the same reason, mysticism and asceticism were treated together under the one title of ascetical theology. In our day every effort is being made to take asceticism and mysticism in their strict meaning and to treat them separately in order not to perpetuate the confusion which has been handed down even to our own time.

276. Taking mysticism as we have explained, we fully agree with A. Goodier when he writes: "There is no true mysticism, whatever may be accepted as its definition, without asceticism; and there is no true asceticism, taken in the Christian sense, without at least some deep insight into the vision of God." [5] No matter how the nature of mysticism is explained by the two schools of thought mentioned before, the fact remains that mysticism is not a substitute for asceticism, except in contemplation, where God takes the initiative, and He alone decides about the time, the duration, the place of contemplation. In everything else the ascetical life of the soul continues unchanged. Mysticism does not change human nature, nor are temptations a thing of the past. St. Paul had been already the recipient of many and sublime mystical graces, revelations, visions, raptures during which he was "caught up to the third heaven," but he was still being "buffeted" by a sting of his flesh, and he found it necessary to beseech the Lord repeatedly that it might depart from him. God's answer finally came, not as a deliverance, but as an en-

[5] *Ascetical and Mystical Theology*, p. 4.

couragement to perseverance in his struggle: "And He said to me: My grace is sufficient for thee: for power is made perfect in infirmity." [6] To resist and overcome temptations, the mystic has no other means at his disposal than the ordinary ones of the ascetical life. The mystic may feel not only the sting of his flesh but also the pride of his spirit for the greatness of his graces. He meets with misunderstanding, suspicion, false accusations, and persecutions. In all these situations the ordinary virtues must be practiced, and genuine Christian asceticism becomes the real test of mysticism.[7]

QUIETISM

277. Quietism (from the Latin *quies,* repose, inactivity) is a false mysticism and also the negation of asceticism. The basic principle of quietism, as taught by Michael Molinos (1627–96), is that perfection consists in absolute passivity of the soul. Any kind of human effort or activity would interfere with God's work. "Let God act," is the quietist motto or guiding principle, meaning: "Let God alone do everything."

278. The inactivity recommended by quietists extends not only to mental prayer but also to spiritual life in general. Once and for all time, the soul should make an act of complete passivity. This done, no other act of virtue is required, no resistance to temptations is demanded. The perfection of the quietists consists in self-annihilation, mystical death, and transformation and absorption into the divine substance.

[6] II Cor. 12:2–10.
[7] The concept of mysticism will be developed in a second volume, *The Mystical Life.* For other meanings of mysticism and asceticism, see P. P. Parente, *Quaestiones de mystica terminologia,* Catholic University, 1941.

279. The period most afflicted with quietist and semi-quietist doctrines was the seventeenth century. We shall mention here the best-known quietist writers of that period.

Benedict Fytche, a Capuchin (d. 1610), is the author of the *Regula perfectionis; seu breve totius vitae spiritualis compendium.* It was printed in 1625 and had many editions. It was condemned by the Holy See in 1689 together with about eighty other works of the same nature. The full title of the English translation of this book gives an idea of its quietist character: *The Rule of Perfection, containing a brief and conspicuous abridgement of all the wholle spiritual life, reduced to only this point, of the Will of God.*

Vita dello Spirito ove s'impara a far orazione, ed unirsi con Dio, by Antonio de Rolas, secular priest (Madrid, 1620). In this work the author recommends to all persons alike a mental prayer without acts, except preparatory ones.

Father John Falconi of the Order of Mercy, who died in Madrid, 1638, and for a time after his death was honored as Venerable, wrote a *Lettre à une fille spirituelle; Lettre à un Religieux,* etc. His writings were condemned in 1688.

Pratique facile pour élever l'âme à la contemplation, by Francis Malaval, a layman of Marseilles, 1664. This work was soon attacked by Father Paolo Segneri, S.J., in his *Sette principii,* 1680, and was finally put on the Index, 1688.

280. Father of modern quietism is the Spanish priest Michael Molinos, who lived for twenty years in Rome, where in 1675 he published his principal work, the *Guida spirituale.* One of the latest English translations of this condemned work is that by K. Lyttelton, *The Spiritual Guide*, 1888. Molinos was very clever in presenting his quietist doctrines, by employing words and expressions consecrated by use but giving them a new meaning. It is not surprising, therefore, that praise and admiration for his work were expressed by some cardinals and inquisitors of the Holy Office. One of those cardinals, on becoming Pope Innocent XI, offered Molinos living quarters in the Vatican.

Dominican and Jesuit theologians protested against the new doctrine of Molinos, noting how under his influence entire religious communities were disregarding long established ascetical exercises, vocal prayer, confession, and so on, in order to waste their time in quietist inactivity or Molinist contemplation. At the outset, Molinos' protectors turned against the accusers; one of them, the Jesuit Father Paolo Segneri, narrowly escaped being condemned to death. But Molinos' hpyocrisy did not last very long. His doctrine was examined and condemned by the same Pope Innocent XI in 1687. Sixty-eight condemned propositions, taken from his writings, express his quietism.[8] There was more than doctrinal error in the charges brought against Molinos. These were proved true during his trial, which lasted for two years. He confessed his immorality, and was condemned to life imprisonment. Nine years lated he died, reconciled with the Church.

281. About the same time, the works on mysticism written by the Oratorian Pietro Matteo Petrucci, bishop of Iesi and later cardinal, 1686, were proscribed by the

---

[8] Denz., 1221–88.

Inquisition because affected by quietism. Petrucci submitted at once and resigned his bishopric in 1688.

Other quietists of this period were Joseph Beccarelli of Milan, who retracted, and the Barnabite Francis Lacombe, who was Mme. Guyon's director. His work *Orationis mentalis analysis* was condemned in 1688.

282. The first of the sixty-eight condemned propositions of Michael Molinos expresses the fundamental idea of quietism: "Man must annihilate his powers, and this is the inward way." [9] If a person wishes to be active, he assumes a divine prerogative and offends God, who wishes to act alone; hence every action, even in prayer, is an imperfection. "Let God act" means, therefore, remain passive and let God do everything. By such inactivity, the soul goes back to its origin, the divine nature into which it is then transformed (prop. 5), in such a manner that the two are one, and so God lives and reigns in us (*ibid.*). Quietist passivity requires not only that no positively good actions of any kind be performed, but also that no resistance be offered to temptations of any sort (prop. 35, 37, 38, 41, 42). Nothing must be asked from God; neither preparation nor thanksgiving is necessary for Holy Communion; no examination of conscience is advisable in the passive quietist state (prop. 9, 15). The soul reaches a point where even the petitions of the Lord's Prayer become objectionable (34). Confession, theology, philosophy, are not for those who belong to the "inward way" (59), because through their acquired contemplation they have reached a state of perfection where no sin is possible (57). Having attained true deification and

[9] *Ibid.*, 1221.

impeccability, the soul is not obliged to internal obedience to any superior, except God (65).

283. Quietism found a fervent apostle in the French woman Mme. Guyon de la Mothe (1648–1717), whose writings amount to forty volumes, all of them condemned, 1689. Her principal works are: *Moyen court et très facile de faire oraison* (Grenoble, 1685); *Les torrents spirituels; Opuscules; Sa vie.* The last one appeared in an English translation by J. T. Allen, in 1898, as *Autobiography of Mme. Guyon,* 2 vols. Also in English, had previously appeared: *A Short Method of Prayer and Spiritual Torrents,* translated by Marston, 1875. Francis Lacombe and Fénelon became her directors, but she succeeded in making them her own disciples and associates after filling them with her notions. Mme. Guyon was not a woman of culture nor was she endowed with good judgment. Her writings prove that she was satisfied with any argument even when evidently false. But she had winning manners and knew how to make partisans. Preaching of God and prayer all the time, she made piety fashionable among the ladies of the Court in France. Her piety, however, was pure quietism, abandonment carried to the extreme, namely, to annihilation and spiritual death.

She demands obedience from Fénelon, who was her director: "Your littleness," she writes, "must extend itself to the point of believing and practising what God causes to be said to you by me" (Letter 108). She promises Fénelon the rank of a general in the great army of mystics, called "Michelins" or soldiers of St. Michael, who will establish the reign of true prayer on earth. In this mystical army that she intended to build there were offices of all sorts, a novice master, an almoner, a jailer, a street porter, a flower-girl, a portress, a female sacristan, etc. She has been defined, "half-saint, half-lunatic," entirely quietist, but with some concessions toward activity. She marks the transition from pure quietism to semi-quietism.

284. Pure quietism, like that of Molinos, is fostered by pantheism and theosophy. It is a heretical system, based on false principles, leading to fatal consequences for morality. It is entirely opposed to Scripture and tradition, wherein a Christian is urgently exhorted to work out his salvation, cooperating with the grace of God which is offered to all. Activity, efforts, endeavor, are demanded everywhere in the Scriptures of both the Old and the New Testament. The Decalogue, the performance of spiritual and corporal works of mercy enjoined by Christ as a necessary practice of a living charity, the precept of praying without intermission, the necessity for a Christian to deny himself, to take up his cross daily and to follow Christ in the practice of virtue, the necessity of hearing the Church and fulfilling her precepts, all this means inward and outward activity, cooperation with God, not supine indolence and passivity.

285. The Protestant doctrine of justification without good works is fundamentally quietist, with the difference that where a quietist makes an act of complete indifference or passivity, a Protestant makes an act of faith, and both expect God to do everything else with regard to their sanctification. For this reason Protestants have rejected partly or entirely the sacramental system. The necessity and utility of good works had been denied by Master Eckhart (1260–1327). His influence on Protestant thought, and the affinity of his doctrine with Protestant ideas, are well known. He affirms that the outward act is not com-

manded by God, because it is neither good nor supernatural, and that God loves the soul, not the exterior act.[10]
The doctrine about sin as taught by early Lutherans and
by Michael Molinos can be found already in Master Eckhart's fourteenth and fifteenth condemned propositions.[11]
Master Eckhart's principles were based on false mysticism
and on quietism. He admitted not only a transformation
and absorption of the just man into the divine substance,
but also a perfect identity of nature and operation with
God, including the creation of heaven and earth and the
generation of the Word.[12]

286. Before leaving modern quietism, we must mention one of its common and well-known variations, semi-
quietism. Introduced by Mme. Guyon, it found its noblest
victim, for a time, in the Archbishop of Cambray, François de Salignac Fénelon.[13] Here, too, we have the fundamental idea of waiting for divine action. When a practical
resolution must be made, no action will be taken until
we are urged thereto by God. The soul will wait, doing
nothing at all until the Spirit of God sets it in motion. This
is acting by impulsion or fancy. The other idea, which is
characteristic of semi-quietism, is the idea of "pure love."
According to Fénelon, pure love is a perfect charity that
excludes all fear, all hope, all thought of self-interest or
advantage. It is an exaggerated disinterested love. It is
exaggerated, because it is carried so far that one becomes
indifferent with regard to his own eternal salvation. Hope,
like faith, remains with us in this life. Charity does not

---

[10] *Ibid.*, 516, 517, 519.
[11] *Ibid.*, 514, 515.
[12] *Ibid.*, 510, 513.
[13] His semi-quietist doctrine of pure love is found in his booklet entitled
Explications des maximes des saints sur la vie intérieure, Paris, 1697.

exclude hope but increases it. Even though the doctrine of "pure love" does not go to the absurd and immoral extremes of quietism, inactivity and passivity are encouraged by the fact that a person becomes indifferent about his eternal salvation and depends exclusively on the action of the Holy Spirit for doing anything.

Fénelon's doctrine was attacked by Bossuet and was subsequently condemned as erroneous by Pope Innocent XII in 1699.[14] The seventeenth century is thus characterized by quietism and semi-quietism till its very end. Fénelon humbly and nobly submitted to the condemnation of his doctrine and retracted. The doctrine of "pure love," however, has preserved its appeal, as of something heroic in spiritual life, on simple souls that do not stop to consider its fatal consequences and implications.

287. The quietists of the seventeenth century merely continued and enlarged quietist doctrines disseminated in earlier centuries. The Alumbrados of Spain in the sixteenth and seventeenth centuries were quietists professing doctrines received from the pantheistic Brethren and Sisters of the Free Spirit. According to these early quietists, perfection consists in complete absorption in God. The human will becomes identical with the divine. There is, then, no need for sacraments, for law, for worship, and the person can indulge in carnal desires without staining the soul. The Beguines and the Beghards, condemned in the Council of Vienne (1311–12), and the Fraticelli, condemned a few years later (1318) by Pope John XXII, professed quietist doctrines with regard to Christian perfection. We had occasion to report their doctrine when treating of Christian perfection.

[14] Denz. 1327–49.

288. At the very beginning of Christianity, Antinomian Gnostics emancipated the soul of the "spiritual," who had acquired intuitive knowledge, from all obligations of moral law. The Messalians or Euchites (the "praying ones") had only one duty, to pray. Prayer, according to them, makes a person entirely free. Passions and evil inclinations are no more.

The tendency of quietism has always been to reduce Christian duties and obligations to a minimum; the quietists of the seventeenth century reduced those obligations to passivity, to nothing.

289. Quietism is also characteristic of pantheistic Brahmanism and Buddhism. The goal, the perfection, to be attained in these religions consists in imperturbable tranquillity, absolute indifference, self-annihilation. The *apatheia*, the supreme perfection of Greco-Roman Stoicism, consisted in becoming emotionless, indifferent, imperturbable. Any indulgence in sensuality was licit as long as the body alone was concerned. The soul, on account of the acquired *apatheia*, could not be defiled. Identical were the views of Michael Molinos in this regard.

The danger of quietism is ever present. Quietist tendencies exist even today. Pope Pius XII warns against such tendencies in his encyclical, *Mystici Corporis Christi* (§ 101), of June 29, 1943: "Just as false and dangerous is the error of those who try to deduce from the mysterious union of all with Christ a certain unhealthy quietism. They would attribute the whole spiritual life of Christians and their progress in virtue exclusively to the action of the Divine Spirit, setting aside and neglecting the corresponding work and collaboration which we must contribute to this action."

CHAPTER XXII

RETREATS

290. Retreats are considered here only as means of perfection and an extraordinary ascetical practice. Retreats were purposely omitted from the enumeration of the general means of perfection for two reasons. First, because we take as general means only the daily or quasi-daily spiritual exercises, the frequent use of which is apt to keep the soul in continual practice. Retreats are made ordinarily once a year; in this respect they belong to the category of extraordinary means of perfection. The second reason is that all the essential parts of a retreat, as prayer, reading, meditation, instructions, examination of conscience, have been explained.

291. Something, however, must be said on the subject of retreats before closing this treatise on ascetical life. It is true that retreats occur only once a year, but their blessings are long-lasting and are often felt throughout the year. In addition to divine grace, the efficacy of retreats is owing principally to a systematic coordination of all the ordinary means of perfection. Their combined action, applied for several days without intermission, cannot fail to produce a profound effect on the soul.

292. Recollection is another factor contributing to the efficacy of retreats. Without recollection we cannot have prayer, meditation, examination of conscience. The silence and solitude, are the proper atmosphere of a retreat.

Recollection implies cessation of ordinary business and study, of reading, not in harmony with the retreat or with the work of each day. It means restraint of the eyes and generally mortification of the senses. He who makes a retreat, no matter where, imitates Christ who went into the desert to pray, to fast, and to be tempted by the devil.[1] As far as a person's soul is concerned, he goes into solitude to remain there alone with God. The voice of God is heard ordinarily in solitude, not in the whirlwind of distractions. His voice is like "a whistling of a gentle air"; [2] it is not heard easily amid the deafening noise of ordinary life. In solitude, the soul that was like a desert will bloom like a garden in spring.

293. Retreats are one of the most beautiful and effective forms of asceticism in modern times. The practice of retreats as a series of days spent in recollection, prayer, and penance, is certainly a very old one. It was in use among the prophets of the Old Testament. The example of Christ, who spent forty days in the desert alone, praying and fasting, has inspired pious souls in every century to spend several days annually in complete retirement and recollection. The Christian hermits of the early centuries spent most of their life in the solitude of the desert in prayer and other ascetical exercises. It was in the solitude of a cave near Subiaco that St. Benedict relegated his young life until the day that he came out as a spiritual guide of souls, a leader of men, a patriarch of Western monasticism. St. Francis of Assisi and his companions often retired to some hermitage in the mountains of Umbria and Tuscany, where they gave themselves up to

[1] Matt. 4:1–11.
[2] III Kings 19:11–13.

prayer and mortification. It was a kind of forty days' retreat, a *quadragesima*. It was during one of his last retreats
on Mount Alverno that St. Francis received the seal of
divine approval in his mortal body, the sacred stigmata
of Christ.

294. Retreats of this kind were not made according to
a definite method. The fervor and devotion of the individual were the only guide. St. Ignatius Loyola, as we
have seen before, gave new impetus to mental prayer,
and with his little book, *The Spiritual Exercises,* he restored and encouraged the practice of retreats. He coordinated the various means of perfection into a logical
system. He explained each one of those ascetical means
to be employed in a retreat and gave practical advice
regarding their use. His explanations and directions are
specific with regard to meditation and examination of
conscience. His book remains the most practical guide for
anyone who makes or gives a retreat even today. St. Ignatius leaves a certain amount of initiative to both retreat
master and retreatant; this element of freedom makes the
book always up-to-date.

295. St. Ignatius' retreat or *Exercises* lasts four weeks,
nearly thirty days. These four weeks are commonly divided into three parts, corresponding to the three ways:
the purgative, the illuminative, and the unitive way. The
first week begins with the meditation on the end of man
and creatures and continues with six meditations on sin:
the sin of the angels; the sin of Adam; personal sins; the
infinite malice of mortal sin; effects of mortal sin; number
and greatness of our personal sins. Several exercises are
given on the punishments of sin: exercise on hell; application of the senses on the same subject; exercises on death;

on the particular judgment. The first week aptly closes
with meditations on the prodigal son, his wanderings, his
return. The return of the prodigal son is a touching figure
of the happily concluded purgative way. This is done
with a good, thorough confession, usually a general confession of the whole life or of a good portion of it.

296. As in real ascetical life, so also in St. Ignatius'
retreat, in which we have a condensed version thereof, the
illuminative way is the longest and the most exposed to
temptations. The second and third weeks belong to the
illuminative way. The first week had for its aim to destroy
the empire of sin in the soul and to reform life: *Deformata
reformat*. The example given by Christ in His life and during His Passion are the real form of Christian living. The
life of Christ becomes the ordinary subject of meditation
during this second period. Christ's life is the model. It
must be studied that we may conform our own life to it:
Reformata conformat. The meditations on the Holy Eucharist and those on the sufferings and death of Christ
on the Cross have the special purpose of strengthening all
good resolutions taken during the second week: *Con-
formata confirmat*.

297. The fourth week introduces the soul into the unitive way. It is a new life, a transformation; *Confirmata
transformat*. It begins with the meditation on the Resurrection; continues with the glorious life of Christ on earth
after his Resurrection, with His Ascension; finds its climax
in the meditation on the love of God, and on the prayer
Suscipe. Two meditations on one of the sweetest devotions, the devotion to the Blessed Virgin Mary, close the
retreat.

298. We do not pretend to have traveled within a short month of spiritual exercises the long, difficult, and laborious road to the unitive way and to Christian perfection. It is only a framework that must be built up, a sketch that must be worked out. The book of the *Spiritual Exercises* is, therefore, not a complete handbook of asceticism. Ascetic principles and practices are largely and wisely employed and lucidly explained but only as far as necessary. It has been said that St. Ignatius had a particular case in view, the making of the great choice, choosing a vocation. He deals with a crisis. Yet, if the *Spiritual Exercises* deal admirably well with such critical situations, should we not be able to find there an answer and a solution to ordinary difficulties of everyday interior life?

299. St. Ignatius leads his retreatant on ordinary ascetical ways. He has a practical aim, to give to the King of heaven another subject, another soldier, another missioner. He leaves it to God to endow His soldier or His missioner with mystical graces, if it be His good pleasure. No doubt, St. Ignatius was put on guard against any exaggeration of the unitive ways by the false mysticism of the Alumbrados that swept over parts of Spain in his day. Besides, he could teach only what we must and can do to acquire perfection with the ordinary grace of God, and this is asceticism. He demands especially personal effort, active cooperation of the retreatant, great initiative. Passivity does not enter in asceticism, it has no part in a retreat. The spirituality of St. Ignatius is pugnacious. He had been a soldier and a knight. The love of God, the love and attachment to Christ, must be made manifest in fighting against the enemies of God that are in us, fighting against bad habits and evil inclinations. As a former soldier he demands strict discipline in spiritual life. All this is diametrically opposed to the lazy passivity of the quietists.

300. The practice of making a retreat was made obligatory by rule by the Jesuits first among all active religious orders. St. Ignatius prescribed a retreat of thirty days for every member of the Order before the admission to the vows. It was later introduced also during the third probation. Little by little the custom of repeating the retreat in an abridged form of eight full days, every year, prevailed. The sixth General Congregation of the Jesuits, held in 1608, prescribed this yearly retreat of eight days. Encouraged by the Holy See (Pope Paul V, 1606), other religious orders and even seculars soon adopted the same practice.

301. St. Charles Borromeo promoted the practice of retreats among priests and among seminarians before their sacred ordinations. For this purpose he built what he called an *asceterium*, a retreat-house and put it under the direction of his Oblates. St. Francis de Sales and St. Vincent de Paul extended and encouraged the practice in France. Retreat-houses for lay people were opened all over Catholic Europe.

302. From the middle of the seventeenth century, synodal statutes everywhere began to prescribe that the clergy should make a retreat from time to time. The ever-growing outward activity of the clergy in our dynamic age makes it imperative to devote a few days every year to a spiritual renewal. Canon law requires that all secular priests make a retreat every three years at least.[3] It is according to the spirit of the law that the retreat be made every year. This is the laudable practice observed in most dioceses of the United States.

[3] *Code of Canon Law*, can. 126.

BIBLIOGRAPHY

BIBLIOGRAPHY

Works of General Interest

BARDY, G. La vie spirituelle d'après des écrivains des trois premiers siècles. Paris, 1935.

BUCHBERGER, M. Lexicon fuer Theologie und Kirche; 10 vols. Freiburg-Br., 1930–38.

BUTLER, C. Western Mysticism; 2nd ed. London, 1927.

CABROL, F. La prière des premiers chrétiens. Paris, 1929.

CATHOLIC ENCYCLOPEDIA; 16 vols. New York, 1907–14.

DURRANT, C. S. Flemish Mystics and English Martyrs. Benziger, 1925.

GUIBERT, J. de. Documenta ecclesiastica christianae perfectionis studium spectantia. Rome, 1931.

JAEGER, P. de. An Anthology of Mysticism. London, 1935.

MARECHAL, J. Studies in the Psychology of the Mystics. Benziger, 1927.

MARTINEZ, F. L'ascétisme chrétien pendant les trois premiers siècles. Paris, 1913.

POURRAT, P. Christian Spirituality; 4 vols. London, 1922–30.

ROUET DE JOURNEL-DUTILLEUL. Enchiridion asceticum; 2nd ed. Freiburg-Br., 1936.

VILLER, M. La spiritualité des premiers siècles chrétiens. Paris, 1930.

—— and others. Dictionnaire de spiritualité. I, A-C, Paris, 1937–39.

ZOECKLER, O. Askese und Moenchtum; 2 vols. Frankfurt a M., 1897.

Hagiography

One of the principal sources of information in the study of ascetical and mystical theology is the lives of the saints and servants of God recorded in the Scripture of both Testaments and in authentic biographies. To this class belong that collection of the *Acta martyrum* which is recognized as authentic by modern critics, the official process of beatification and canonization of the servants of God, and the not yet completed collection of the *Acta sanctorum* of the Bollandists. The third edition of this vast collection (Paris, 1863–69) extends only to the month of October. The series, still in progress, had reached the middle of November by 1930. The number of hagiographies is so great in our own age that a complete enumeration of them is out of the question. Only such hagiographies should be taken into consideration as are known to be historically accurate. Modern biographies are, generally speaking, more reliable than those of former days on account of the progress of historical studies in our generation.

A list of hagiographies can be found in *Biographia Catholica* by H. Korff (Freiburg-Br., 1927). A list of autobiographies is found in *Dictionnaire de spiritualité*, I, 1152–58. Classics of this kind are the following:

AUGUSTINE, St. Confessionum libri tredecim.

BENSON, E. H. Confessions of a Convert. London, 1928.

BORSI, Giosué. Spiritual Colloquies of Giosué Borsi. Kenedy, 1918.

CAPITANIO, Blessed Bartholomea. Scritti spirituali. Modena, 1904.

CHRISTINE, Lucie. The Spiritual Journal of Lucie Christine; ed. by A. Poulain. Paris, 1920.

DUPANLOUP, F. Journal intime. Paris, 1902.

FOUCAULT, Charles de. Ecrits spirituels. Paris, 1923.

GEMMA Galgani, St. Lettere ed estasi; ed. by Father Germano, C. P., 1909.

JAEGEN, Hieronimus. Das Mystische Gnadenleben. Trier, 1934.

LESEUR, Elizabeth. Journal. Paris, 1915.

OLIVAINT, P. Journal de ses retraits; 2 vols. Paris, 1872.

SORAZU, Angeles. Autobiografia. Valladolid, 1929.

THERESA OF JESUS, St. Life. Several translations and editions. One of the best English translations is that by David Lewis, first published in 1870; 4th ed., 1911.

THERESA of the Infant Jesus, St. Autobiography. Kenedy.

TONIOLO, Joseph. Le mie memorie religiose. Milan, 1919.

Periodicals

ETUDES CARMELITAINES. Published since 1911.
LA VIE SPIRITUELLE. Paris, since 1919.
REVUE D'ASCETIQUE ET DE MYSTIQUE. Toulouse, since 1920.
REVIEW FOR RELIGIOUS. St. Marys, Kansas, since 1942.
VIDA SOBRENATURAL. Salamanca, since 1921.
VITA CRISTIANA. Florence, since 1929.
ZEITSCHRIFT FUER ASZESE UND MYSTIK. Innsbruck, since 1926.

Patristic Sources

APOSTOLIC FATHERS; Funk-Bihlmeyer edition. Tuebingen, 1924.
English translations: Ante-Nicene Fathers; American edition
by A. Menzies, 10 vols. The Apostolic Fathers are in Vol. I.
Scribners, 1926. Apostolic Fathers I, in Loeb Classical Library.
Putnam.
CLEMENT of Rome, St. Epistle to the Corinthians. This work con-
tains exhortations to charity, humility, obedience, and other
virtues.
DIDACHE, The. It contains the doctrine of the two ways which is
found also in the Epistle of Barnabas and in the Apostolic
Constitutions, Bk. VII, chaps. 1–2.
IGNATIUS MARTYR, St. Mystical concepts and expressions appear
for the first time in Christian literature in the epistles of St.
Ignatius, especially in the epistle to the Romans and in that to
the Ephesians.
HERMAS. Pastor. In this work, symbolic and mystical elements are
introduced for the purpose of instruction and exhortation.
Such elements are visions and similitudes.

AMBROSE, St. De virginibus; De virginitate; De institutione vir-
ginis; De viduis; De officiis ministrorum; De bono mortis; De
fuga saeculi. PL, 14–17.

ATHANASIUS, St. Life of St. Anthony; Letters to Dracontius, Orsien-
sus, Amunis, and to the monks. PG, 18.

AUGUSTINE, St. Soliloquia; Confessiones; De doctrina christiana;
De civitate Dei; Epistula 211; many of his sermons. PL, 32–47.

BASIL the Great, St. The Holy Spirit; Rules at length; Rules in
abridgment. PG, 29–32.

BENEDICT OF NURSIA, St. Regula monasteriorum. PL, 66.

BENEDICTUS Anianensis. Codex regularum. PL, 103.

CASSIAN, John. Collationes; De institutis coenobiorum et de octo
principalium vitiorum remediis, libri XII. PL, 49.

CHRYSOSTOM, St. John. On the Priesthood; most of his celebrated
homilies. PG, 48–64.

CLEMENT of Alexandria. Paedagogus; Stromata; Quis dives salve-
tur. PG, 9.

CLIMACUS, St. John. Scala Paradisi. PG, 88.

CYPRIAN, St. De Dominica oratione; De habitu virginum; De bono
patientiae; De zelo et livore; De lapsis; De mortalitate; Epistulae. PL, 4.

CYRIL of Jerusalem, St. Catechetical lectures. PG, 33.

DIADOCHUS Photicensis. De perfectione spirituali capita C. PG, 65.

DIONYSIUS, Pseudo-Areopagita. De divinis nominibus; De mystica
theologia; De caelesti hierarchia; De hierarchia ecclesiastica;
Epistulae. PG, 3–4.

EVAGRIUS Ponticus. Antirrheticus (only in Latin and Syriac frag-
ments); Maxims for Coenobites (Centuriae); The Monk.
PG, 40.

GREGORY the Great, St. Expositio in librum Job, sive Moralium
libri XXXV; Liber regulae pastoralis curae; Dialogorum libri
IV; Homilies; Sermons; Epistulae. PL, 75–79.

GREGORY Nazianzen, St. Orationes; especially Oratio II apologetica. PG, 35–38.

GREGORY of Nyssa, St. Life of Moses; Life of St. Macrina; On Virginity. PG, 46.

JEROME, St. Letters (especially to Eustochium, to Nepotianum, to
Paula, to Marcella, to Lea, to Blesilla, to Asella); Vita Pauli
monachi; Vita Malchi; Vita beati Hilarionis. PL, 22–30.

MACARIUS Aegyptius. Epistula ad filios. Ed. Wilmart in the Revue d'ascetique et de mystique, 1920.

MAXIMUS Confessor, St. Scholia in Opera St. Dionysii Areopagitae; De variis locis difficilibus SS. Dionysii et Gregorii Theologi; Liber asceticus; Capita de caritate; Epistula I. PG, 90–91.

NILUS (abbot), St. De monastica exercitatione; De voluntaria paupertate. PG, 79.

ORIGEN. Homiliae in Canticum canticorum; Selecta in Psalmos; De oratione; Commentaria; De principiis. Ed. De La Rue, 1733–59, in PG, 11–17. *See* Das Vollkommenheitsideal des Origenes by W. Voelker. Tuebingen, 1931.

PALLADIUS. The Lausiac History; The History of the Monks; Life of St. John Chrysostom. PL, 73.

TERTULLIAN. De oratione; Ad martyres; De velandis virginibus; De patientia; Apologeticum; De testimonio animae. PL, 1–3.

Medieval Authors

ADAM Scotus. De triplici genere contemplationis; De tripartito tabernaculo. PL, 198.

ALBERT the Great, St. Commentarii in Dionysium Areopagitam. Under his name were formerly other works; e.g., De adhaerendo Deo; Paradisus animae. Ed. A. Borgnet. Paris, 1890–99.

ANGELA of Foligno, Blessed. Her visions, revelations, doctrine, etc., are found in the critical edition, Angèle de Foligno, by Paul Doncoeur, in Dictionnaire de spiritualité. Paris, 1937.

ANSELM, St. Liber meditationum et orationum. PL, 158. English translation, Meditations and Prayers. London, 1872.

BEATRIX a Nazareth. Van seven manieren van Minne, or, On the seven degrees of love. Louvain, 1926.

BERNARD of Clairvaux, St. Sermones in Cantica canticorum; De consideratione; De diligendo Deo; De gradibus humilitatis et superbiae. PL, 182–84.

BERNARDUS Cassinensis. Speculum monachorum; ed. Wolter. Friburg, 1901.

BONAVENTURE, St. Itinerarium mentis ad Deum; Incendium amoris,

seu de triplici via; Soliloquium; Lignum vitae; Vitis mystica;
De sex alis seraphim; De perfectione vitae ad sorores; Regula
novitiorum. Quaracchi, 1882–92, V and VIII.

BRIDGET of Sweden, St. Revelationes Sanctae Birgittae Sueciae. In
eight books. Rome, 1628.

CATHERINE of Siena, St. The Dialogue. London, 1907. Letters. New
York: Dent, 1905.

CAVALCA, Dominic. Specchio dei peccati; Specchio della Croce;
Disciplina delli spirituali (ed. Levasti); Mistici del duecento
e del trecento (Milan, 1935).

CLOUD OF UNKNOWING, The. By an unknown author of the fourteenth century; ed. McCann. London, 1924.

DIONYSIUS the Carthusian. His complete works (40 vols.) contain
commentaries on Cassian, Climacus, Pseudo-Areopagite, etc.
Opera omnia, Montreuil, 1896–1913.

FRANCES of Rome, St. Life and visions. See Acta sanctorum,
March 9.

FRANCIS of Assisi, St. Opuscula. Ed. crit., Quaracchi, 1904. Actus
Beati Francisci, freely translated into Italian, became the
celebrated Fioretti, of which several English translations have
been made. Benziger, 1927, etc.

GERSON, John. De theologia mystica speculativa et practica; De
monte contemplationis; De elucidatione scholastica mysticae
theologiae; De meditatione; De perfectione cordis; De dis-
tinctione verarum visionum a falsis; De probatione spirituum;
De conscientia scrupolosa; De tentationibus diaboli; De oratione et suo valore, etc. Opera omnia; 5 vols. in folio. Antwerp,
1706.

GERTRUDE the Great, St. Insinuationes divinae pietatis; ed. Oudin,
1875. Typical of her mysticism is the devotion to the Sacred
Heart.

GUIGO II. Scala claustralium. PL, 184.

GULIELMUS a St. Theodorico. Epistula ad fratres de Monte Dei; De
contemplando Deo; De natura et dignitate amoris; Medita-
tivae orationes. PL, 184.

HARPIUS, Henry. Theologia mystica. Based entirely on Ruysbroeck.
Cologne, 1538.

HILDEGARD, St. Scivias (i.e., scire vias Domini vel lucis); Liber divinorum operum simplicis hominis. PL, 197.

HUGH of St. Victor. De vanitate mundi; Soliloquium de arrha animae; De laude caritatis; De amore sponsi ad sponsam; De meditando; etc. Rouen, 1648.

HYLTON, Walter. The Scale of Perfection, a devout treatise, compiled by Master Walter Hylton of the Song of Angels; The Cell of Self-Knowledge. New edition (1908–10), London, New York.

JULIANA of Norwich. Sixteen Revelations of Divine Love; 4th ed. New York: Gorham, 1911.

LAWRENCE, Justinian. De compunctione cordis et complanctu christianae perfectionis; De vita solitaria; De contemptu mundi; De perfectionis gradibus; De incendio divini amoris. Opera omnia. Venice, 1751.

MECHTILDIS of Hackeborn, St. Das Buch geistlicher Gnade. Leipzig, 1503. A critical edition in Latin (Paris, 1875–77) comprises also the revelations of St. Mechtildis of Magdeburg: Revelationes Gertrudianae et Mechtildianae.

NICHOLAS of Cusa. De docta ignorantia; Apologia doctae ignorantiae; De visione Dei. Leipzig, 1933.

RICHARD of St. Victor. Benjamin minor; Benjamin maior, seu de gratia contemplationis; Expositio in Cantica canticorum. PL, 196.

RICHARD Rolle. The Fire of Love; the Amending of Life; The Form of Perfect Living; etc. Selected works: London, 1930.

RUYSBROECK, Blessed John. Werken van Jan van Ruusbroec, 6 vols. Ghent, 1858–69. Selected works in English: New York, 1925.

SUSO, Blessed Henry. Das Buechlein der ewigen Weisheit. In English: The Little Book of Eternal Wisdom. Benziger, 1889.

TAULER, John. Sermons; ed. Vetter. Berlin, 1910.

THOMAS Aquinas, St. Ascetical and mystical questions are treated in most of his works. These questions were systematically arranged by T. a Vallgornera in his work, Mystica theologia divi Thomae. Turin, 1927.

THOMAS a Kempis. In the first edition of his works (Utrecht, 1475), the Imitation of Christ was not mentioned. Life and writings. Freiburg: Herder, 1903–22.

VINCENT Ferrer, St. De vita spirituali; Sermons. Augsburg, 1729.

Modern Times

ALVAREZ de Paz. De vita spirituali eiusque perfectione. Lyons, 1602.

BAKER, Augustine. Sancta Sophia; translated as Holy wisdom. London, 1932.

BELLARMINE, St. Robert. De ascensione mentis in Deum per scalas creaturarum; De aeterna felicitate sanctorum; De gemitu columbae sive de bono lacrymarum; De arte bene moriendi; Opuscula ascetica. Pustet, 1925. Life and Work of Blessed Robert Bellarmine; 2 vols. London, 1928.

BELLINTANI da Saló, Matthias. Pratica dell'orazione mentale. New ed., Assisi, 1932–34.

BERULLE, Peter de. Œuvres complètes. Paris, 1657. Migne, 1856.

BLOSIUS, Louis. Spiritual Works; 6 vols. Benziger, 1926.

BRANCATI de Laurea. De oratione christiana. Rome, 1675.

CAMBI da Salluzzo, Bartolomeo. Luce dell'anima; Paradiso dei contemplativi. Selected works in Sarri's Il sacro cigno. Florence, 1924.

FRANCIS de Sales, St. Introduction to a Devout Life. Benziger, 1925. Library of St. Francis de Sales; 7 vols., 1908–25. Treatise on the Love of God; Letters to Persons in Religion; Letters to Persons in the World; Catholic Controversy; Mystical Explanation of the Canticle of Canticles; Conferences.

IGNATIUS Loyola, St. Spiritual Exercises; ed. Lattey. Herder, 1928. Constitutions of the Society of Jesus; Letters; Autobiography, in Monumenta Ignatiana. Madrid, 1903 ff.

JANE FRANCES de Chantal, St. Selected Letters. Kenedy, 1918. Her Exhortations, Conferences, and Instructions. Loyola University Press, 1929.

JOHN of the Cross, St. Critical edition of the original works by Father Silverio. Burgos, 1929–31. The Ascent of Mount Carmel; The Dark Night of the Soul; The Living Flame; The Spiritual

Canticle; Precautions; Counsels and Maxims; Spiritual Letters; Poems. Ed. Zimmerman. London, 1906 ff.

LALLEMANT, Louis. Spiritual Doctrine of Father Louis Lallemant. New York, 1885.

LANCICIUS, Nicholas. Select Works. London: Burns & Oates, 1884.

LaPUENTE (De Ponte). Meditations on the Mysteries of Our Holy Faith. Benziger, 1916.

LE GAUDIER, Antonius. De natura et statibus perfectionis. Turin, 1903.

LOUIS of Granada. Libro de la oración y meditatión; Memorial de la vida christiana. Critical ed. by Cuervo in 14 vols. Madrid, 1906.

MARGARET MARY Alacoque, St. Œuvres; 3 vols., ed. Gauthey. Paris, 1915.

MARY of the Incarnation, Ven. Life, written by her son D. Martin. Paris, 1677.

OLIER, Jean Jacques. Œuvres. Migne, 1856.

PETER of Alcantara, St. Tratado de la oración y meditatión. In Etudes Franciscaines, 1923.

PHILIP NERI, St. Lettere, rime e detti memorabili. Florence, 1922.

RODRIGUEZ, Alphonsus. Practice of Christian Perfection; 3 vols. Chicago, 1929.

SCUPOLI, Lawrence. Il combattimento spirituale. English: The Spiritual Combat. Many editions.

SEGNERI, Paul. Manna dell'anima. English: Meditations for a Year; 4 vols. London, 1879.

SUAREZ, F. The Religious State: Digest of the Doctrine of Suarez, by Humphrey. London, 1884.

SURIN, J. Catéchisme spirituel; les fondements de la vie spirituelle. Paris, 1930.

THERESA, St. Critical edition of all her works in the original, by Father Silverio; 9 vols. Most important are: The Book of Her Life; The Way of Perfection; The Mansions; Relations; Foundations; Letters. Several translations in English are available.

THOMAS a Iesu. Tratado de la oración mental; De contemplatione divina libri VI; De contemplatione acquisita. Opera omnia, 1684.

THOMAS of Bergamo. Fuoco d'amore. Augsburg, 1682.

TRONSON, L. Forma cleri. Œuvres; 2 vols. Migne, 1857.

ZACCARIA, St. Antonius M. Le Lettere e lo spirito religioso di S. Antonio M. Zaccaria; ed. Pontremoli. Rome, 1909.

VINCENT de Paul, St. Complete works in 14 vols. Paris, 1920–25. St. Vincent de Paul and Mental Prayer. Benziger, 1925. Some Counsels of St. Vincent de Paul. Herder, 1914.

More Recent Times

ALPHONSUS LIGUORI, St. Among his many ascetical and mystical works must be numbered: Homo apostolicus; Praxis confessarii; Le glorie di Maria; Massime eterne. Complete ascetical works. English translation by Grimm; 22 vols. Benziger, 1886–92.

ARINTERO, John. Cantar de los Cantares, exposition mistica, 1919. Cuestiones misticas; 2nd ed., 1920. Evolutión mistica; 2nd ed., 1921. La verdadera mistica traditional, 1925. Grados de oración; 4th ed., 1935.

AURELIANUS a Smo. Sacramento. Cursus asceticus; 3 vols. Ernaculam, India, 1917–19.

BOSSUET, J. B. Instruction sur les états d'oraison. Paris, 1897. Méditations sur l'evangile. Doctrine spirituelle de Bossuet. Paris, 1908.

CAFASSO, Blessed Joseph. Meditazioni, Istruzioni per esercizi spirituali al clero; 2 vols., 1892–93.

CHAIGNON, P. Meditations for Secular Priests; 2 vols. Benziger, 1906.

CLARET, Ven. A. M. La escala de Jacob; Avisos; Reglas de espiritu; several other shorter works.

DEVINE, A. Manual of Ascetical Theology. Benziger, 1902. Manual of Mystical Theology, 1903.

EYMARD, Blessed J. Le très Saint Sacrament; 4 vols.

FABER, F. W. All for Jesus; Growth in Holiness; Blessed Sacrament; Creator and Creature; At the Foot of the Cross; The Precious Blood; Spiritual Conferences. Many editions.

FARGES, A. Mystical Phenomena. London, 1926. Ordinary Ways of Spiritual Life. New York, 1927.

FENTON, Joseph C. The Theology of Prayer. Bruce, 1939.

GABRIELE di S. Maria Maddalena. La mistica Teresiana. Florence, 1934. S. Teresa maestra di vita spirituale, 1935. La contemplazione acquisita, 1938.

GARRIGOU-LAGRANGE, R. Christian Perfection and Contemplation. Herder, 1937.

GOERRES, Joseph. Christliche Mystik; 4 vols., 1836–48.

GOODIER, Alban. Ascetical and Mystical Theology. London, 1938.

GUIBERT, Joseph de. Theologia ascetica et mystica. Rome, 1939.

HERTLING, L. Lehrbuch der aszetischen Theologie. Innsbruck, 1930. Theologiae asceticae cursus brevior. Rome, 1939.

HODGSON, G. English Mystics. London, 1922.

JOSEPH a Spiritu S. Cursus theologiae mystico-scholasticae; 6 vols. Seville, 1710–40.

LAMBALLE, F. Eud. La contemplation. Paris, 1911.

LAMBERTINI, Prospero (Benedict XIV). De servorum Dei beatificatione et beatorum canonizatione. Venice, 1788.

LEVASTI, A. I mistici; 2 vols. Florence, 1925; Mistici del Duecento e del Trecento. Milan, 1935.

LIBERMAN, Ven. Francis. Instructions sur la vie spirituelle, sur l'oraison; L'oraison affective; Ecrits spirituels. 1891. Lettres spirituelles; 3 vols. 1874.

MANNING, H. E. Internal Mission of the Holy Ghost; Glories of the Sacred Heart. London, 1876. Eternal Priesthood. Baltimore.

MARMION, Columban. Christ the Life of the Soul. Herder, 1935. Christ in His Mysteries; Christ the Ideal of the Monk.

MAUMIGNY, R. de. Pratique de l'oraison mentale; 2 vols., 1905.

MESCHLER, Mauritius. Das Leben unseres Herrn, 1890. Die Gabe des hl. Pfingstfestes; Geistesleben; Aszese und Mystik; Three Fundamental Principles of the Spiritual Life. Herder, 1912. Life of Our Lord Jesus Christ, the Son of God, in Meditations; 2 vols. Herder, 1924. Garden of Roses of Our Lady. London, 1907.

NEWMAN, J. H. Meditations and Devotions; Works; 40 vols. Longmans, 1874–1921.

OLGIATI, F. La pietá cristiana, esperienze ed indirizzi. Milan, 1935.

PAGANI, John P. The Science of the Saints in Practice; 3 vols. 1860.

PARENTE, Pascal P. Quaestiones de mystica terminologia. Catholic University (Washington), 1941.

PINAMONTI. Opere spirituali. Venice, 1762.

POULAIN, Augustine. The Graces of Interior Prayer. Herder, 1910.

ROSMINI, Antonio. Massime di perfezione o Lezioni spirituali; Storia dell'amore; Manuale dell'esercitatore. All these works under the title: Ascetica. Milan, 1840. Epistolario ascetico; 5 vols. 1911–13.

SCARAMELLI, G. B. Direttorio ascetico; Direttorio mystico. English tr. 4 vols. New York: Kelly, 1902.

SCHMIDT, H. Organische Aszese. Paderborn, 1939.

STOLZ, Anselm. The Doctrine of Spiritual Perfection. Herder, 1938.

STURZO, Luigi. The True Life. St. Anthony Guild Press, 1943.

TANQUEREY, A. The Spiritual Life. Desclée, 1930.

TEODOROWICZ, Joseph. Mystical Phenomena in the Life of Theresa Neumann. Herder, 1940.

ZIMMERMAN, Otto. Lehrbuch der Aszetik; 2nd ed. Freiburg, 1932.

INDEX

ABC of spiritual life, 92
Acta martyrum, 256
Acta sanctorum, 46, 256
Actio vitalis, 142
Actions: heroic, 154; naturally good, 26 f.; *see* Virtue
Affections, 115; *see* Prayer
Albigensians, 21
Alexander VIII (pope), 25
Aloysius Gonzaga, St., 65
Alphonsus Liguori, St., 57, 173
Alumbrados, 243
Alvarez de Paz, 73, 149
Ambrose, St.: on prayer, 59; on reading, 226
Angels, the two, 166
Anthony, St.: temptations of, 110
Antinomian Gnostics, 244
Apatheia, 30, 244
Aridity, 90, 150
Arintero, 141
Aristotle, 124 f., 140
Art of arts, 174, 176
Ascent, the soul's, 69
Ascetic: meaning of the word, 3-5; nature of, 6; object of, 18; relation to dogma and moral, 7-9; relation to mystical theology, 6, 13, 231
Ascetical theology: definition of, 6; importance of, 11 f.; methods of, 9; various acceptations of, 13
Asceticism: false, 20; Stoic, 181 f.; true, 184 ff.
Athanasius, St., 4, 110, 229
Athleticism, the Christian, 4, 182 f.
Augustine, St.
   activity of love, 194
   bodily pleasures, 102 f.
   commandment and counsel, 43
   human love, 26

Augustine, St. (*continued*)
   kinds of vice, 100
   modesty, 103
   on object of charity, 197
   perfection of charity, 42
   power of love, 51
   spiritual progress, 51
   on temptation, 103, 105
Austerities, 96 f.

Balma, Hugo de, 71, 120
Basil, St., 53, 58, 159
Beghards and Beguines, 37, 243
Beginners in spiritual life, 76 ff.
Benedict XIV (pope), 129
Benedict of Nursia, St., 82, 246
Bernard, St., 61, 64, 144
Berulle, de (cardinal), method of, 11, 89
Bishops, 217
Bona (cardinal), 149
Bonaventure, St., 71, 87
Borromeo, St. Charles, 250
Bossuet, 243

Cajetan, 35
Cassian, 71, 107
Cassiodorus, 124
Catharists, 21
Catherine of Siena, St., 135
Chantal, St. F. J. de, 151
Charisma, 163
Charity, 31-36, 38-42, 127; *see* Love
Charles Borromeo, St., 250
Chastity, 186 f.
Christ: imitation of, 53 f.; model of perfection, 52
Christian life, the, 18-27
Cicero, 140
Cisneros, Garcia Ximenes de, 88
Clement I, St. (pope), 183

267